Course

ASSESSMENT

Chapter Tests

- **Reading**

- **Writing**

- **Sentences and Paragraphs**

- **Grammar, Usage, Mechanics**

HOLT, RINEHART AND WINSTON

A Harcourt Classroom Education Company

Austin · New York · Orlando · Atlanta · San Francisco · Boston · Dallas · Toronto · London

STAFF CREDITS

EDITORIAL

Director
Mescal Evler

Manager of Editorial Operations
Bill Wahlgren

Executive Editors
Robert R. Hoyt
Emily G. Shenk

Project Editor
Cheryl L. Christian

Writing and Editing
Barbara Scroggie Knaggs
Rebecca Bennett
David Knaggs
Paige M. Leavitt
Kim Soriano, *Editorial Assistant*

Copyediting
Michael Neibergall, *Copyediting Manager;* Mary Malone, *Senior Copyeditor;* Joel Bourgeois, Elizabeth Dickson, Gabrielle Field, Jane Kominek, Millicent Ondras, Theresa Reding, Kathleen Scheiner, Laurie Schlesinger, *Copyeditors*

Project Administration
Marie Price, *Managing Editor;* Lori De La Garza, *Editorial Operations Coordinator;* Thomas Browne, Heather Cheyne, Diane Hardin, Mark Holland, Marcus Johnson, Jill O'Neal, Joyce Rector, Janet Riley, Kelly Tankersley, *Project Administration;* Gail Coupland, Ruth Hooker, Margaret Sanchez, *Word Processing*

Editorial Permissions
Janet Harrington, *Permissions Editor*

ART, DESIGN AND PHOTO

Graphic Services
Kristen Darby, *Manager*

Image Acquisitions
Joe London, *Director;* Tim Taylor, *Photo Research Supervisor;* Rick Benavides, *Assistant Photo Researcher;* Elaine Tate, *Supervisor;* Erin Cone, *Art Buyer*

Cover Design
Sunday Patterson

PRODUCTION
Belinda Barbosa Lopez, *Senior Production Coordinator*
Simira Davis, *Supervisor*
Nancy Hargis, *Media Production Supervisor*
Joan Lindsay, *Production Coordinator*
Beth Prevelige, *Prepress Manager*

MANUFACTURING
Michael Roche, *Supervisor of Inventory and Manufacturing*

Printed in the United States of America

ISBN 0-03-056382-8

1 2 3 4 5   085   04 03 02 01 00

Table of Contents

Communications

Table of Contents

Sentences and Paragraphs

Grammar, Usage, and Mechanics

About These Tests

Every chapter in your *Elements of Language* Pupil's Edition has an accompanying Chapter Test in traditional format. The Answer Keys for these tests are located in a separate booklet, *Test Answer Keys*.

Part 1

Communications

The Part 1 tests include assessment for both the Reading and the Writing Workshops. You may choose to administer the Reading and Writing Workshop tests separately or as one test after students have completed the chapter.

In the **Reading Workshop** test, students read a passage, respond to short-answer questions, and complete a graphic organizer. The passage is in the mode that students have just studied, and the questions and the graphic organizer assess students' proficiency in the chapter's Reading Skill and Reading Focus.

The **Writing Workshop** test provides a passage containing problems or errors in several or all of the following areas: content, organization, style, grammar and usage, and mechanics. Students demonstrate their understanding of the mode of writing and their revising and proofreading skills by revising the essay and correcting the errors. A Revising Guidelines page reminds students of the chapter skills and the basic requirements of the chapter writing mode.

To help students complete the Writing Workshop tests, you may want to give them photocopies of the following page, which lists symbols for revising and proofreading.

Part 2

Sentences and Paragraphs

The Part 2 tests provide assessment for each major section within the Sentences and Paragraphs chapters. Students complete exercises similar to those in the Pupil's Edition. These exercises test students' mastery of the key concepts taught in the chapters.

Part 3

Grammar, Usage, and Mechanics

The Part 3 tests provide assessment for the rules and key concepts taught in the grammar, usage, and mechanics chapters in the Pupil's Edition. Students demonstrate their mastery of the instruction by completing a variety of tests that are similar to the exercises in the Pupil's Edition.

Symbols for Revising and Proofreading

The following symbols will help you revise and correct the passages in the Writing Workshop tests.

SYMBOL	DEFINITION	EXAMPLE
‿ℓ	Delete word.	The girl smiled ~~at me.~~ ℓ
∧	Insert.	The girl smiled ∧. *at me*
∕ ⎯	Replace a word.	I found the ∕~~book.~~ *record*
≡	Set in capital letters.	Does karen like fish? ≡
∕	Set in lowercase.	Does Karen ∕Like ∕Fish?
∨	Insert apostrophe.	Its his dog.
"∨ ∨"	Insert quotation marks.	It's his dog, he said.
⊙	Insert period.	If she goes, I go ⊙
∧	Insert comma.	If she goes ∧ I go.
⊙	Insert colon.	Pick a color ⊙red, blue, or green.
∧	Insert semicolon.	We went ∧ she stayed.

Reading Workshop: Personal Reflection

DIRECTIONS Read the following passage, and answer the questions in the right-hand column.

Reaching the Heights

As we pulled into the parking lot of the amusement park, my hands perspired and my mouth was dry. I had foolishly agreed to go on every ride my children did, and now I had to make good on my promise.

A fear of heights has plagued me throughout my life. If I stand on a balcony, I know it will collapse. When I climb a ladder, my heart races like a freight train hurtling down the tracks. Riding in an elevator with glass walls dooms me to white-knuckled terror from the moment it leaves the ground.

When we entered the gates of the park, I knew it was too late to back out. My children would have understood, but they would have been disappointed. I would have to overcome my fear. They led the way toward the back of the park and a small roller coaster that ended in a fifty-foot drop through water. Oh, great, I thought, only one quick drop! The entire ride I dreaded the fated moment. When we reached the top of the drop, I made the mistake of looking down. The safety bar was a lifeline. I cemented my hands to it and closed my eyes as the car catapulted down the tracks. Seconds later, the cold spray told me the ordeal was over. I took a deep breath and stepped out of the car.

"What next?" my teenage son asked.

I wanted to suggest the merry-go-round, but I knew better. Within minutes, we were boarding the cable cars that ran the length of the park. As we swung out over the crowds in what seemed to be an endless journey, my stomach crept into my throat. I swallowed

1. According to the first paragraph, how was the writer feeling? What makes you think so?

_____

_____

_____

_____

_____

2. Do you think the writer enjoyed the roller coaster ride? How can you tell?

_____

_____

_____

_____

_____

my fears and looked at the clear blue sky instead of the miniature
people below.

At the center of the park stood a ride that vowed to hurtle us
through star-dotted blackness like an out-of-control asteroid careening
through space. The line was long, which gave me too much time to
anticipate what could happen. At regular intervals, signs announced,
"Caution: Those with back or heart conditions should avoid this
ride." Each time I saw a sign, I quickly evaluated my health. My back
ached a little, perhaps from standing in line for two hours, or perhaps
it was something serious. My heart pounded. Could I have an undi-
agnosed life-threatening condition? Should I risk my life by going on
this ride? I almost left the line. However, my children tugged at my
shirt, saying, "Come on, Dad." I had survived two rides; perhaps I
could try one more.

I stepped onto the loading platform with the sense that I was
entering a nightmare from which there was no escape. The attendant fastened me into the cart, and I slid into the darkness. With a
lurch the cart flew forward, and I attempted to keep my eyes open
as we charged through space. I don't think I breathed until we
careened into the unloading station. When the attendant released
the safety mechanism, I peeled my fingers from the crossbar. I wob-
bled on shaky legs to the exit.

As normal breathing returned, I realized that I had ridden the
three rides I had feared the most. My children looked at me with
new respect. I looked at myself a little differently, too: skydiving
might be something to explore. Why not?

3. What narrative details in this paragraph reveal the writer's conflicting emotions about the ride?

_____

_____

_____

_____

4. What descriptive details does the writer use to show his fear?

_____

_____

_____

_____

_____

5. Do you think the writer will be able to face other fears more easily? Explain.

_____

_____

_____

_____

_____

DIRECTIONS Use the details from the passage you have just read to complete the graphic organizer below.

Identifying Descriptive Details

▶ FIGURATIVE DETAILS	▶ SENSORY DETAILS	▶ FACTUAL DETAILS
1. my heart races like a freight train hurtling down the tracks	**1.** mouth was dry	**1.** pulled into the parking lot
2.	**2.**	**2.**
3.	**3.**	**3.**
4.	**4.**	**4.**

Writing Workshop: Personal Reflection

DIRECTIONS Use the following guidelines to help you revise and correct the essay on the next page.

THE INTRODUCTION SHOULD

- start with an interesting opener
- provide background information
- hint at the meaning of the experience

THE BODY SHOULD

- include details that make the events, people, and places memorable
- include descriptions of the writer's thoughts and feelings
- include only events that are necessary to the experience
- relate the events so that they are easy to follow

THE CONCLUSION SHOULD

- state the significance or meaning of the experience

REMEMBER TO

- ❑ use participial phrases to add sentence variety
- ❑ ensure subject-verb agreement in sentences that contain intervening phrases

Writing Workshop: Revising and Proofreading

DIRECTIONS The following personal reflection was written in response to this prompt:

> **Write about the first time you participated in a particular activity.**

The essay contains problems in content, organization, style, and grammar.

- Use the space between the lines to revise the essay and correct the errors.
- If you cannot fit some of your revisions between the lines, rewrite the revised sections on a separate piece of paper.

Becoming a Part of the Lake

Kayaking in a mountain lake in Alaska looked extremely interesting in the travel brochures, but I had never kayaked before. At summer camp, I had learned to row a small boat and assumed that kayaking would be similar. I had no idea that it would allow me to become part of the lake in a new way.

We arrived at the mountain lake early in the morning. We were dressed in warm, waterproof clothing. We prepared ourselves for the water. We grabbed our paddles and headed to our kayaks. We eased our two-person kayak into the still water. My friend and I learned to paddle in unison. Our guide helped us.

> **a.** Problem with sentence construction

Once the occupants of all ten kayaks developed a rhythm in their paddling strokes, the silence of the lake filled our ears. The gentle splash of the paddles were all we heard as our kayaks slid through the silver water.

> **b.** Problem with subject-verb agreement

Without making a sound, we approached the beach and the eagle. A bald eagle glided onto the beach not far from us. Our guides

> **c.** Problem with order

quietly instructed us to paddle to the shore. Unaware of our kayaks, the majestic bird strutted down the shore as we watched it from one hundred feet away.

Soon our guides reminded us that we needed to return to the bus, so we went back across the lake. Ahead of us a salmon came out of the water. After we drew up on the shore, we got out of our kayaks and returned to the bus.

d. Problem with descriptive details

The eagle and the salmon didn't seem to notice us because the kayaks were so quiet.

e. Problem with conclusion

Reading Workshop: Comparison-Contrast Article

DIRECTIONS Read the following passage, and answer the questions in the right-hand column.

ITV Classrooms and Traditional Classrooms

For one hour a day, I teach a class of thirty students, even though my room has only fifteen desks. In fact, I have not even met all of my students in person, because some live hundreds of miles away. Instead, we meet every day through interactive television (ITV).

My ITV classroom differs from my traditional classroom in a number of ways. To begin with, my ITV classroom looks different. It requires microphones, cameras, and TV monitors so that the teacher and students can communicate. Without this equipment, holding class is difficult or impossible. Traditional classrooms, by contrast, rely on person-to-person interaction.

Teaching an ITV class also requires different skills from teaching a traditional class. Teachers must be familiar with the interactive technology and equipment and must be ready to resolve any technical problems that arise during class. Teachers must also structure their lessons differently because teacher-student interaction is more difficult over the television. Typical discussion periods or question-answer sessions are not as easy to moderate, so teachers must ask questions and call directly on students to elicit responses. Because of the technical linkages, teachers may also have to wait longer for responses. ITV teachers must also develop different strategies for reinforcement and review because they cannot rely as easily on visual cues to tell them when students are bored or confused.

Not only teachers but also ITV students have to make adjustments. Students must get used to the technology and feel comfortable speaking to the teacher and other students during the session. In addition, because students get less personal contact with the

1. What is the main idea of this article?

_____

_____

_____

_____

_____

2. What aspects of the traditional classroom and the interactive television classroom does the second paragraph contrast?

_____

_____

_____

_____

_____

3. What details about teaching in a traditional classroom are implied (not directly stated) in the third paragraph?

_____

_____

_____

_____

teacher than in a traditional classroom, they must learn to work independently and to communicate with the teacher outside class via e-mail or telephone. ITV students cannot depend on the teacher to look over their shoulders and remind them to do the work either. As a result, they have to be more self-motivated and self-disciplined.

An ITV classroom and a traditional classroom provide different learning environments and offer different challenges and opportunities to teachers and students. ITV opens new doors for students who want access to different courses, but traditional classes provide security and the high level of teacher support that helps many students learn successfully.

4. What supporting details does the writer give for the idea that ITV students have to make changes in the way they learn?

_____

_____

_____

_____

_____

5. What method has the author used to organize this essay?

_____

_____

_____

_____

_____

DIRECTIONS Use the ideas and information in the third paragraph to complete the graphic organizer.

Identifying Main Idea and Supporting Details

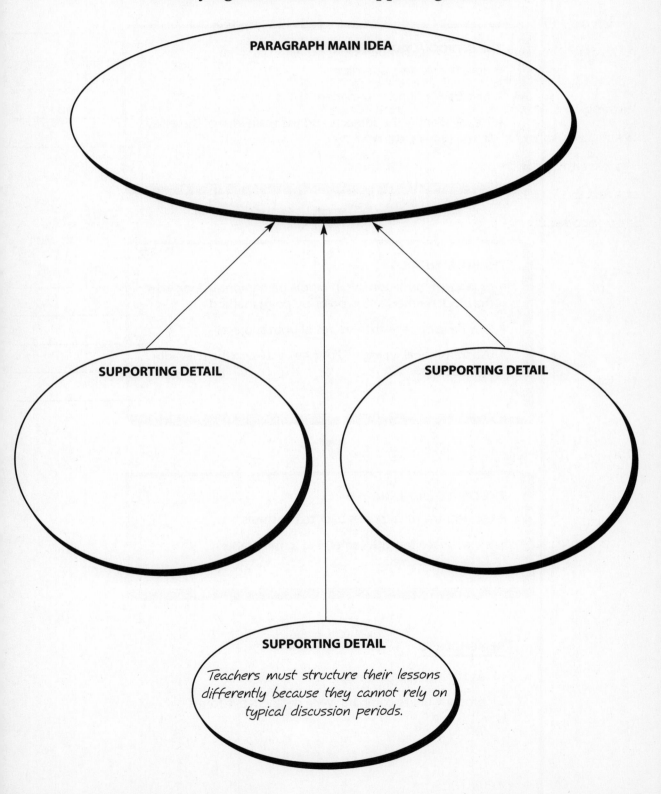

PARAGRAPH MAIN IDEA

SUPPORTING DETAIL

SUPPORTING DETAIL

SUPPORTING DETAIL

Teachers must structure their lessons differently because they cannot rely on typical discussion periods.

Writing Workshop: Comparison-Contrast Essay

DIRECTIONS Use the following guidelines to help you revise and correct the essay on the next page.

THE INTRODUCTION SHOULD

- grab the reader's attention

- give background information

- clearly identify the subjects and the main idea of the essay in the thesis statement

THE BODY SHOULD

- organize information into multiple paragraphs using either the block method or the point-by-point method

- fully develop relevant features of both subjects

- use transitional words and phrases between the relevant features

THE CONCLUSION SHOULD

- connect the main points back to the thesis

- leave the reader with something to remember

REMEMBER TO

- ❑ use only precise adverbs

- ❑ properly utilize comparative and superlative forms

Writing Workshop: Revising and Proofreading

DIRECTIONS The following essay was written in response to this prompt:

> **Write a comparison-contrast essay about elements of nature.**

The essay contains problems in style, organization, and grammar.

- Use the space between the lines to revise the essay and correct the errors.
- If you cannot fit some of your revisions between the lines, rewrite the revised sections on a separate piece of paper.

Restoring the Forests

A forest fire destroys 45 percent of Yellowstone National Park. A

windstorm sweeps through the western Adirondack Mountains,

damaging or destroying at least 30 percent of the trees on 104,000

acres. The damage sometimes seems overwhelming.

> **a.** Problem with thesis

Both forest fires and windstorms occur really regularly. Monica

> **b.** Problems with adverbs

Turner, a landscape ecologist at the University of Wisconsin at

Madison, explains that every one hundred to three hundred years

the natural fire pattern in Yellowstone "includes a hot crown fire

that replaces the whole forest." Windstorms follow a very similar

pattern. Experts estimate that in the Adirondacks major windstorms

occur approximately every thirty years. Clearly, both windstorms

and forest fires are part of forests' life cycles.

Areas opened up by forest fires and windstorms grow again,

bringing back many of the plants that grew before, as well as those

> **c.** Problem with order within paragraph

that had been eliminated by the shade of the forest canopy.

Windstorms allow growth of shade-tolerant trees, creating more diversity in the forest, and forest fires expose sections of bare soil, which is essential for certain pine trees to seed.

Both fires and windstorms bring benefits to wildlife. The open areas created by fires and windstorms allow for new growth, which feeds deer and moose. Windstorms knock over dead trees. These felled trees provide shelter for many species, from insects to small mammals.

d. Problem with transitions

Forest fires and windstorms are a natural part of the ecosystem. These natural phenomena are similar in that they both help keep forests healthy and benefit wildlife. While we should be careful not to cause forest fires, when a forest needs to be renewed, the combination of a lightning bolt and dry weather is the most quickest method. Windstorms also cannot be prevented; they will come in their natural cycle and are also a means of forest renewal.

e. Problem with superlatives

Reading Workshop: Cause-and-Effect Article

DIRECTIONS Read the following passage, and answer the questions in the right-hand column.

The Darkened Sky

Shortly before noon on September 5, 1881, the sky turned black over four counties in the Thumb District of Michigan. As strong winds blew from the southwest, the air filled with smoke and ash. By the time the smoke had cleared, two thousand square miles of forest had burned. The causes of this disaster were both human and natural.

Some of the conditions for the massive fire were created when lumber camps lined the shores of Lake Huron around 1850. Because the tall, straight trunks of native white pines and the bark from hemlocks were the only commercially useful parts of the trees, lumberjacks carelessly left the unwanted trunks and branches to accumulate on the forest floor. Then, in 1871, a fire swept through the tops of the trees in the forests of the Thumb District so quickly that it killed trees without entirely consuming them. As a result, the remaining charred stumps added to the already huge piles of highly flammable kindling, piles as deep as twelve to fifteen feet.

Weather conditions also contributed to the disastrous fire. No significant rain had fallen for almost two months, and most wells and streams were dry. Cracks criss-crossed the dry earth. Had it rained prior to the fire, the moist ground could have helped prevent its spread. Furthermore, high southwesterly winds up to forty miles per hour were recorded in the southern area of the forest. These hurricane-force winds not only knocked down large trees, but also tore roofs from buildings and lifted people off their feet.

People lit the match that touched off the flames. To clear their land of tree stumps and brush piles, settlers in the Thumb District burned them. Strong winds and dry conditions did the rest.

1. Does the writer begin the essay with cause or effect? Explain.

   _____
   _____
   _____
   _____
   _____

2. What words in the second paragraph signal cause-and-effect relationships?

   _____
   _____
   _____
   _____
   _____

3. How did lack of rain contribute to the disastrous fire?

   _____
   _____
   _____
   _____
   _____

4. What cause-and-effect relationship can you infer from the last two sentences of the fourth paragraph?

   _____
   _____
   _____
   _____

As the horrific fire approached, people took refuge in cleared fields, in wells, and in Lake Huron. The wind fanned the flames so quickly that, according to some accounts, horses racing away from the flames were overtaken and engulfed. The dense smoke prevented many settlers from finding shelter. As a result, 280 people perished, thousands of people were left homeless, and countless domestic and wild animals died.

5. What organizational pattern does this essay use?

_____

_____

_____

_____

_____

DIRECTIONS Use the ideas and information in the article you just read to complete the graphic organizer.

Analyzing Cause-and-Effect Structure

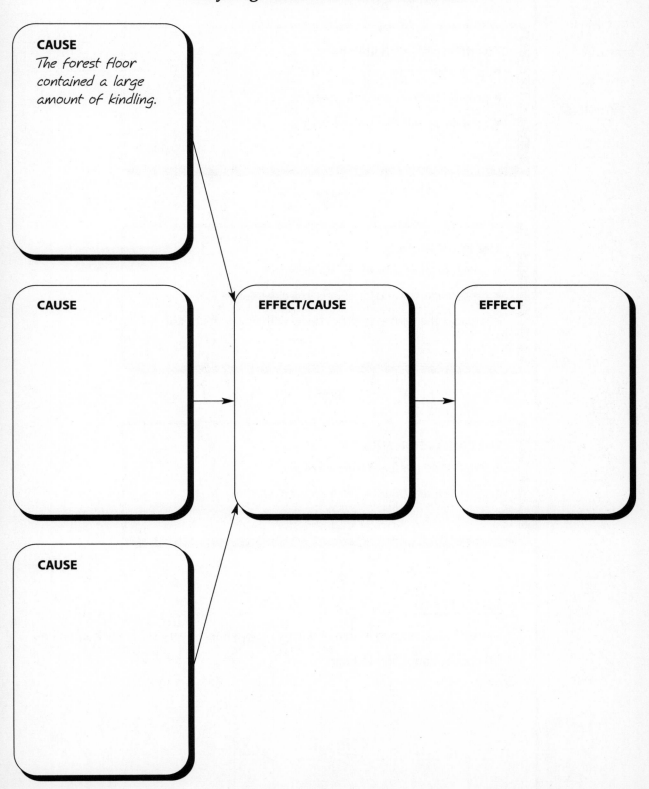

CAUSE
The forest floor contained a large amount of kindling.

CAUSE

CAUSE

EFFECT/CAUSE

EFFECT

Writing Workshop: Cause-and-Effect Explanation

DIRECTIONS Use the following guidelines to help you revise and correct the essay on the next page.

THE INTRODUCTION SHOULD

- hook your audience
- provide background information
- contain a clear thesis statement

THE BODY SHOULD

- develop cause-and-effect statements
- present causes and/or effects in a clear sequence
- support the causes and/or effects with adequate detail

THE CONCLUSION SHOULD

- remind the reader of the thesis
- provide a reasonable and logical conclusion

REMEMBER TO

- ❑ use infinitives and infinitive phrases as openers to vary sentence beginnings
- ❑ correct dangling modifiers

Writing Workshop: Revising and Proofreading

DIRECTIONS The following essay was written in response to this prompt:

> **Write a cause-and-effect essay about an environmental topic.**

The essay contains problems in style, organization, and grammar.

- Use the space between the lines to revise the essay and correct the errors.
- If you cannot fit some of your revisions between the lines, rewrite the revised sections on a separate piece of paper.

The Dwindling Amazon

The Amazon rain forest of Brazil is a global resource. However, 12 percent of the Amazon has already been cleared for agriculture and logging. Deforestation has been in practice in the Amazon for decades, and it is crucial to identify the local and global negative effects.

> **a.** Problem with hook

One of the most noted consequences of deforestation involves the danger of global warming. Carbon dioxide in the atmosphere is considered a major cause of global warming. The Amazon—also known as the "lungs of the world"—absorbs an immense amount of carbon dioxide and then releases oxygen. Less forest means more carbon dioxide in the air. Huge fires are set to clear the land for argricultural use. These fires also contribute to excess carbon dioxide and, consequently, to global warming. A result of global warming could be plant and animal extinction on a massive scale. Coastal flooding, salt water intrusion, increases in severe storms, and droughts are problems associated with global warming.

> **b.** Problem with sentence beginnings

Another important environmental function of the Amazon could be diminished by deforestation. The forests redistribute heat, cooling the tropics and warming cooler regions. Water from the rain forests evaporates into the atmosphere and creates clouds that cool the region. The clouds also reflect sunlight back into the atmosphere to warm cooler regions.

As land is cleared, Brazilians lose their homes, food, medicine, and culture. The four hundred tribes who live in the Amazon are gradually being pushed out. Locally, deforestation affects the Brazilian people.

c. Problem with organization within paragraph

Deforestation ruins habitats for animals. Species are becoming extinct at one thousand times the natural rate. Housing almost two-thirds of the known organisms in the world, this rate is particularly disastrous. These diverse populations are connected through a set of complex relationships; destroying the habitat of one species may affect species throughout the entire region.

d. Problem with dangling modifier

The clearing of rain forests has several effects.

e. Problem with conclusion

Reading Workshop: Problem-Analysis Article

DIRECTIONS Read the following passage, and answer the questions in the right-hand column.

Fans or Foes?

Last week, in a disturbing display of poor sportsmanship, football fans cheered as the opposing team's quarterback lay flattened on the field with a serious hip injury. Unfortunately, such behavior may be expected of fans of professional sports, but in this case, the quarterback was sixteen years old. The ill-mannered spectators were fans of Portman High School.

In the past, Portman fans had a well-deserved reputation for goodwill and good sportsmanship. Several years ago, for example, PHS students donated time and money to help an athlete from a rival school cover hospital expenses for a sports-related injury. At one time, the PHS pep squad provided half-time refreshments for visiting teams, as well as for the home team. At the state hockey championships three years ago, players, coaches, and fans of rival teams complimented PHS coaches and officials for the gracious behavior of Portman fans.

Since that time, however, many Portman fans have become mean-spirited, even hostile. Last year, four hotheaded fans were ejected from athletic events: two for threatening to injure a soccer referee, one for throwing ice onto the basketball court, and one for verbally abusing a visiting volleyball coach.

Although such behavior reflects poorly on Portman, it also points to a larger problem affecting all levels of athletics, from peewee to professional leagues. This nation has become addicted to winning. And when we cannot win—right here, right now—we feel cheated

1. Why do you think the article begins with a real-life example instead of first stating the problem?

_____

_____

_____

_____

_____

2. Is the generalization in the first sentence in the second paragraph based on sufficient information? Explain.

_____

_____

_____

_____

_____

3. Would it be a hasty generalization to say that many PHS fans exhibited unsportsmanlike behavior? Why or why not?

_____

_____

_____

_____

_____

and look for someone to blame or hurt. Consequently, fans are encouraged to adopt hateful or even violent attitudes toward opponents.

Too often, negative attitudes turn into negative actions, and sportsmanship suffers greatly. Portman fans should strive to regain the goodwill they once had and exhibit the sportsmanship that made their reputation an enviable one. Fans can start by contributing money to send flowers to the injured quarterback and by signing a letter of apology to be printed in the quarterback's school newspaper. PHS fans did not cause the injury to the opposing quarterback last week, but they certainly did further damage to their reputation as sports fans.

4. What is a generalization made in this paragraph?

_____

_____

_____

_____

5. Does this article focus primarily on the problem or on the solution? Why do you think so?

_____

_____

_____

_____

_____

DIRECTIONS Use the ideas and information from the passage you have just read to complete the graphic organizer.

Analyzing Problem-Solution Structure

1. **State the problem.**

2. **Give evidence.**

   ▪ *Last year, four Portman fans were asked to leave athletic events.*

   ▪

   ▪

   ▪

3. **Examine contributing factors.**

   ▪ *Society has lost its perspective on winning.*

   ▪

4. **Propose a solution.**

Writing Workshop: Problem-Analysis Essay

DIRECTIONS Use the following guidelines to help you revise and correct the essay on the next page.

THE INTRODUCTION SHOULD

- catch the audience's attention
- clearly state the problem in the thesis

THE BODY SHOULD

- state at least three key points in a reasoned analysis of the problem
- provide support in each paragraph for the key points
- organize ideas in a way that makes sense

THE CONCLUSION SHOULD

- restate the thesis
- emphasize the seriousness of the problem and its importance to the audience

---

REMEMBER TO

- ☐ avoid redundant or flabby phrases and clauses
- ☐ correct sentence fragments

Writing Workshop: Revising and Proofreading

DIRECTIONS The following problem-analysis essay was written in response to this prompt:

Identify a problem shared by many teenagers.

The essay contains problems in style, content, usage, and grammar.

- Use the space between the lines to revise the essay and correct the errors.
- If you cannot fit some of your revisions between the lines, rewrite the revised sections on a separate piece of paper.

The Great Teenage Sit-In

Today's teenagers are increasingly at risk for chronic diseases because they do not get enough exercise. American Sports Data reported that the number of teenagers who are "frequent fitness participants" has dropped over the years. There are also significant declines in the number of teens who play softball, soccer, and volleyball, even though participation for other age groups has increased. Excessive TV watching and video game use at home may contribute to the couch-potato lifestyle of many teenagers.

> **a.** Problem with thesis statement

In many ways, the school routine actually keeps students from participating in physical activity. The classroom is a setting that requires teenagers to sit throughout most of the school day. Breaks are usually frequent in number and provide teens with an opportunity to stretch and move around, but they do not provide sufficient exercise. School may even affect a student's exercise routine after the last bell has rung: Homework keeps students active.

> **b.** Problem with flabby clause and redundancy

Mandatory physical education classes may help teens keep fit, but few schools require students to take PE classes for all four years of high school. After meeting these class requirements. Teens do not have to participate in any regular physical exercise at school. Although some teenagers participate in school sports or the marching band. The majority of students in a typical school do not.

c. Problem with sentence fragments

Interscholastic sports are often reserved for gifted athletes.

d. Problem with support

By taking advantage of the opportunities that school does provide, as well as developing an active routine, teenagers can maintain a healthy and active personal lifestyle.

e. Problem with conclusion

Reading Workshop: Literary Analysis

DIRECTIONS Read the following passage, and answer the questions in the right-hand column.

Shadowy Evidence in "The Pit and the Pendulum"

Although Edgar Allan Poe's "The Pit and the Pendulum" is rich in ghoulish imagery and horrifying imaginative tortures, the reader discovers only little by little when the story is taking place and what is happening. The tale is of a man's treatment during the Spanish Inquisition, but we know few details about his arrest and trial. We are provided only general information about the story's location. The narrator never refers to himself by name.

The scarcity of background details, however, is not a weakness. Instead, it accounts for much of the story's suspense. As the narrator faces the prospect of being thrown to his death in a pit or of being cut to ribbons by a razor-sharp pendulum, he gives us a great deal of specific information about his state of mind. We share his deprivations, terrors, and final hope in a terrifyingly effective manner.

Poe makes his main character's fear palpable through his masterful use of the first-person point of view. While an omniscient narrator might have identified details of the Spanish Inquisition or described the circumstances of the narrator's arrest, the first-person narrator gives us only what he can logically know. Because his prison is dark, the narrator does not know exactly what he sees or hears. He has difficulty interpreting what is in his own grasp. He can only describe an object he touches as "something damp and hard." He faints in the midst of a particularly horrifying scene. Another recollection is indistinct, and the narrator only "vaguely" remembers the events of his trial—after "much earnestness of endeavor." Because we are limited in what we know, we share in the narrator's confusion.

1. What point do you think the second paragraph is trying to make about Poe's writing style?

_____

_____

_____

_____

2. What could "The Pit and the Pendulum" have been like if Poe had used a different point of view?

_____

_____

_____

_____

3. After reading the third paragraph, what can you determine about the story's narrator?

_____

_____

_____

_____

As the story progresses, the narrator attempts to analyze his situation, "to deduce [his] real condition," but he has little information from which to reason. His limitations create a chilling mystery: What dangers are hidden in the narrator's cell? And where are they? The narrator's answers emerge slowly and painfully as he fades in and out of sleep and a drug-induced stupor, suffering intense torment as he struggles against his growing fear of the unknown.

By playing on one of the most basic of human fears—fear of the unknown—Poe creates a terrifying, suspenseful tale. He does this by focusing exclusively on the thoughts and fears of one character. In the end, Poe shows us that a short story can be effective even when details of setting and plot are part of the story's suspense.

4. How does Poe make his story an effective mystery?

_____

_____

_____

_____

_____

5. What conclusion does the writer make in this paragraph?

_____

_____

_____

_____

_____

DIRECTIONS Use the ideas and information in the literary analysis to complete the graphic organizer.

Analyzing Literary Elements

WHAT LITERARY ELEMENT IS DISCUSSED IN THE PASSAGE?

_____

WHAT IS THE ELEMENT'S FUNCTION?

1. _____

2. *limit the information available to audience*

WHAT IS THE ELEMENT'S EFFECT?

1. _____

2. _____

Writing Workshop: Literary Analysis

DIRECTIONS Use the following revision guidelines to help you revise and correct the errors on the next page.

THE INTRODUCTION SHOULD

- capture the reader's attention by making an interesting comment on the story

- include a thesis statement that provides the title of the story, the author, the literary elements discussed, and the main idea about the elements

THE BODY SHOULD

- support each key point with details from the story

- provide sufficient elaboration for each story detail

- use language that is appropriate for the intended audience, purpose, and tone

THE CONCLUSION SHOULD

- restate the thesis and summarize the key points

- leave the reader with something to consider

REMEMBER TO

- ❏ use complex sentences
- ❏ use quotation marks properly

Writing Workshop: Revising and Proofreading

DIRECTIONS The following essay was written in response to this prompt:

> **Analyze a literary element of a short story. Describe one of the following elements: setting, point of view, character, plot, theme, foreshadowing, or irony.**

The essay contains problems in style and punctuation.

- Use the space between the lines to revise the paper and correct the errors.
- If you cannot fit some of your revisions between the lines, rewrite the revised sections on a separate piece of paper.

Caution and Recklessness in "Trap of Gold"

Louis L'Amour's "Trap of Gold" is a concentrated glimpse into the mind of its hero, a miner named Wetherton. The conflict and action of this story serve one main purpose—to reveal Wetherton's true character. Wetherton "was not and had never been a gambling man" and would not endanger himself or his family's livelihood. Wetherton appears to be cautious, but his actions reveal a dangerous determination that brings him to the brink of a fatal accident.

Although Wetherton is described as conscientious and careful, he is also attracted to the thrill of adventure. He needs his family, but he states that the freedom to explore the desert was "as necessary to him as the other." The miner defines himself by his gold-seeking treks. The miner declares the desert to be "his work, his life, and the thing he knew best."

a. Problem with sentence construction

Despite this adventurous bent, Wetherton stakes his life on a "habit of care and deliberation". In a step-by-step fashion, Wetherton

b. Problem with quotation marks

first locates a vein of gold, inspects its structurally dangerous loca-

tion in a rock mass, and then creates a plan to ensure the safety of his

retreat.

Early into his project, Wetherton says that he can make tons of

money if he just doesn't get greedy or stupid. Indeed, when he finds

an abundance of gold in a rock tower, the gold has a "fascination

that was beyond all reason." Despite his careful nature and prior

knowledge of the irrational lure of gold, he returns to the rock tower

for twenty-two days, even after he knows for certain his mining has

caused the tower to become very unstable. Yet ultimately, his rea-

sonable nature conquers his greed; he stops digging for gold when

the rock structure nearly becomes a death trap.

In Trap of Gold, L'Amour depicts his reasonable hero as

vulnerable to the risks and temptations presented to him.

> **c.** Problem with tone

> **d.** Problem with quotation marks

> **e.** Problem with conclusion

Reading Workshop: Research Article

DIRECTIONS Read the following passage, and answer the questions in the right hand column.

The Durian: A Difficult Delicacy

The wide variety of foods available in the United States reflects a diverse culture. However, most U.S. citizens have not yet been introduced to the durian, a thorny, green fruit about the size of a pineapple that is a delicacy in Southeast Asia.

The durian is little known in Western nations, in part because of its short shelf life. Fresh durians are rarely exported beyond Hong Kong or Singapore. Yet the creamy, golden flesh of the durian is so valued that it is known as "the king of fruits." As early as 1599, a traveler to Malaysia wrote that "it is of such an excellent taste that it surpasses in flavor all the other fruits of the world." Why, then, have U.S. shoppers not demanded a taste?

The answer may lie hidden in an encyclopedia entry that describes the fruit as having a sweet flavor that tastes slightly of garlic. The encyclopedia also notes that when the fruit ripens, it "develops a strong smell." Put more plainly, the exotic taste of the durian is not for the squeamish. One description states that "to those not used to it, it seems at first to smell like rotten onions." The fruit also has been described as having "an abominable stench." In Singapore, government officials find the smell of durians so offensive that "No Durian" signs are posted in public places such as subways, ferries, and taxi stands.

Thai and Malaysian fans of the fruit may prefer to keep the secret of the durian's custard like sweet taste to themselves. *The New York Times* says that fruit sellers in Singapore are particularly concerned about the durian's popularity in Hong Kong. There is a danger that demand could exceed supply, because durian trees can take as long

1. Why does the writer think it is unusual that the durian is not known in the United States?

_____

_____

_____

_____

_____

2. What is the source for this information?

_____

_____

_____

_____

_____

3. Is *The New York Times* a primary or secondary source? Explain.

_____

_____

_____

_____

_____

as fifteen years to bear fruit, compared with only three years for
other popular tropical fruits.

In the United States, the closest one can get to a durian is the
durian candy found in Asian food markets. The tiny jelly globes
smell faintly of an unwashed garbage can, yet the flavor of the
durian is well worth any temporary stench.

4. While in the United States,
how did the writer find out
what durians taste like?

_____

_____

_____

_____

_____

5. Is the article an informal or
formal research article?

_____

_____

_____

_____

_____

DIRECTIONS Use the ideas and information in the passage you have just read to complete the graphic organizer.

Paraphrasing

▶ORIGINAL	▶PARAPHRASE
The durian is little known in Western nations, in part because of its short shelf life. Fresh durians are rarely exported beyond Hong Kong or Singapore. Yet the creamy, golden flesh of the durian is so valued that it is known as "the king of fruits." As early as 1599, a traveler to Malaysia wrote that "it is of such an excellent taste that it surpasses in flavor all the other fruits of the world." Why, then, have U.S. shoppers not demanded a taste?	Because durians ripen quickly, they are not well known in countries that are farther than Hong Kong or Singapore and are seldom shipped outside of this region. The durian is highly prized and is considered to be the most majestic of the fruits. One early traveler to the region stated that the durian's taste is better than that of all other fruits. It is curious that consumers in the U.S. have not asked to try something so delicious.
The answer may lie hidden in an encyclopedia entry that describes the fruit as having a sweet flavor that tastes slightly of garlic. The encyclopedia also notes that when the fruit ripens, it "develops a strong smell." Put more plainly, the exotic taste of the durian is not for the squeamish. One description states that "to those not used to it, it seems at first to smell like rotten onions." The fruit also has been described as having "an abominable stench." In Singapore, government officials find the smell of durians so offensive that "No Durian" signs are posted in public places such as subways, ferries, and taxi stands.	

Writing Workshop: Research Paper

DIRECTIONS Use the following guidelines to help you revise and correct the essay on the next page.

THE INTRODUCTION SHOULD

- grab the reader's attention

- include a thesis statement

- identify the topic and suggest which aspects of the topic are covered

---

THE BODY SHOULD

- support each point with relevant information— summaries, paraphrases, or quotations

- give proper credit for each source

THE CONCLUSION SHOULD

- restate the thesis

- leave the reader with an insight

REMEMBER TO

- ❑ avoid too many long sentences

- ❑ avoid misplaced modifiers

Writing Workshop: Revising and Proofreading

DIRECTIONS The following research paper was written in response to this prompt:

Write a paper that researches a historical event in your state.

The essay contains problems in content, style, and grammar.

- Use the space between the lines to revise the paper and correct the errors.
- If you cannot fit some of your revisions between the lines, rewrite the revised sections on a separate piece of paper.

The Galveston Hurricane

In the nineteenth century, the city of Galveston, Texas, was an influential banking and financial marketplace. Then the hurricane of 1900 destroyed much of the city and reshaped the course of its history.

a. Problem with introduction

Galveston is located on a barrier island in the Gulf of Mexico. In 1900, its deep-water harbor helped make it a center of trade. It was one of the wealthiest cities in the nation. Although the island's highest point stood only 8.7 feet above sea level, the citizens had not thought they needed the protection of a sea wall.

On Friday, September 7, 1900, a steady north wind gained strength, and without satellites and storm-tracking equipment, the 37,000 residents of Galveston could not know that this wind was the first sign of a huge hurricane. On Saturday morning, city residents flocked to the beach who hoped to see the storm roll in. Later in the day, however, a steamboat loosened from its moorings by wind and

b. Problem with sentence length

c. Problem with modifier

water smashed all three bridges that connected the island to the

mainland. The citizens of Galveston were trapped on the island.

A storm with wind speeds estimated at 160 kilometers per hour

covered the entire island with 3 to 5 meters of water. When the

storm finally subsided, over 6,000 people were dead. Like many

hurricane victims, the survivors were in a state of shock. The event

remains the deadliest natural disaster in U.S. history.

The people of Galveston rebuilt their city and constructed a mas-

sive sea wall seventeen feet tall to protect it. Since the hurricane of

1990, however, Galveston has never regained its international status.

d. Problem with
conclusion

Reading Workshop: Persuasive Newspaper Article

DIRECTIONS Read the following passage, and answer the questions in the right-hand column.

Saving the Night Sky

As a child, I would gaze into the night sky for hours, identifying constellations and contemplating the workings of the universe. All the stars seemed so much brighter then. The night sky was a deeper shade of black; but now, the night sky is polluted with excessive outdoor lighting. Light pollution is a very real problem that occurs wherever many people live in a comparatively small space. It comes from many sources: highways, security lights, and billboards to name a few. Excessive outdoor lighting wastes money, causes safety hazards, and prevents astronomers—professional and amateur— from making observations. Most importantly, it intrudes upon the lives of ordinary people every time the sun goes down.

One suburban resident discovered the extent of this intrusion when a service station opened next to his home. He claims that the light spillage from the service station was so great that he could read a newspaper at night in his backyard without turning on any of his own lights. Excessive lighting wastes large amounts of money and fossil fuels. Consider how much electricity and money is wasted across the country; instead of misdirecting light or creating excessive light, we should respect light as a valuable commodity.

The intensity and glare from excessive outdoor lighting also causes safety problems. The human eye can adapt to low light-levels and generally can see adequately in these conditions. However, when it must adjust from a low light-level to a brilliantly lit area, such as an overlit truck stop along a dark highway, a driver's eye can experience temporary blindness that may lead to a serious automobile accident.

1. Is the second sentence a fact or an opinion? Explain.

_____

_____

_____

_____

_____

2. What is the writer's opinion regarding excessive outdoor lighting?

_____

_____

_____

_____

_____

3. What kind of appeal does this anecdote make? Explain.

_____

_____

_____

_____

_____

Urban sky glow—the combined effect of excessive city lights— produces so much glare that it diminishes astronomers' views of the cosmos. The Mount Wilson Observatory sees the stars most clearly when cloud cover obstructs urban glow from nearby Los Angeles. The Goethe Link Observatory near Indianapolis lost much of its research capability to the glare of suburban sprawl years ago. Satellite photographs taken of the United States at night reveal the extent of this problem; light from cities, suburbs, and highways outlines the nation as clearly as a map.

For a problem so vast, the solution is quite simple. Businesses can install deflectors and glare shields on outdoor lighting. Concerned citizens can use an appropriate number of lights with reasonable light output. Replacing energy-gobbling lighting with efficient, low-pressure sodium lamps poses fewer problems for astronomers. If everyone works together to prevent light pollution, maybe then children can once again lie out in the backyard and count the stars.

4. What facts does the author provide to convince readers that light pollution is a problem for astronomers?

_____

_____

_____

_____

_____

5. What kinds of appeals does the writer use in the last paragraph? Explain.

_____

_____

_____

_____

_____

DIRECTIONS Use the ideas and information in the passage you have just read to complete the graphic organizer. Identify each reason included in the article, and then label and indentify the type of support provided for each reason.

Identifying Elements of Persuasion

OPINION: *Excessive outdoor lighting should be diminished.*

REASON:	**REASON:**	**REASON:** *interferes with astronomers' views*
SUPPORT: ■ *anecdote:* ■	**SUPPORT:** ■ ■ *loaded language: may lead to serious automobile accident*	**SUPPORT:** ■ ■

Writing Workshop: Persuasive Essay

DIRECTIONS Use the following guidelines to help you revise and correct the essay on the next page.

THE INTRODUCTION SHOULD

- grab the reader's attention

- include necessary background information

- provide a clear opinion statement

THE BODY SHOULD

- support the opinion statement with adequate reasons and sufficient evidence

- address opposing arguments

- contain emotional appeals, if appropriate

THE CONCLUSION SHOULD

- restate the writer's opinion in an effective conclusion

- include a call to action, if appropriate

REMEMBER TO

- ❑ avoid passive-voice verbs

- ❑ correct double negatives

Writing Workshop: Revising and Proofreading

DIRECTIONS The following persuasive essay was written in response to this prompt:

> **Should students learn a second language?**

The essay contains problems in style, content, usage, and grammar.
- Use the space between the lines to revise the essay and correct the errors.
- If you cannot fit some of your revisions between the lines, rewrite the revised sections on a separate piece of paper.

The Benefits of Learning a Second Language

Learning a second language in high school equips students with

intellectual, linguistic, and cultural tools for success. Before graduat-

ing from high school, students should learn a second language.

> **a.** Problem with hook

Learning a second language has a positive effect on intellectual

growth. The Center for Applied Linguistics asserts that students in

foreign language study programs acquire superior problem-solving

skills and improve overall in school performance. Furthermore,

students may acquire greater creativity, more flexibility in thinking,

and a better ear for listening. Not only do students gain direct access

to additional information, but they also gain a better understanding

of their own language. Students who have studied a second lan-

guage also gain a head start in college language requirements and

score higher on standardized tests conducted in English.

The business world is largely a global marketplace that rewards

those who can communicate in multiple languages. Employers often

recruit bilingual individuals, particularly in areas with large

Hispanic or Asian populations. Even Latin, which not no one speaks

as a first language, may be useful for a career in medicine, botany,

linguistics, or zoology.

| **b.** Problem with double negative |

When another language is learned by students, another culture is

also learned. Students get the opportunity to meet people they

would not otherwise have the chance to know. The more students

from differing backgrounds know about one another, the less likely

prejudices will be held. Insights into a different language and cul-

ture are developed by students through comparisons. Consequently,

bilingual students are better equipped to settle differences and to

find things in common with people from other cultures.

| **c.** Problems with passive voice |

Many students shy away from learning another language

because they believe they don't have the knack for learning this

skill. Some students do find languages more difficult to learn than

other subjects.

| **d.** Problem with argument |

High school students should learn a second language.

| **e.** Problem with conclusion |

Reading Workshop: Persuasive Brochure

DIRECTIONS Read the following passage, and answer the questions in the right-hand column.

Front Panel

Why drive when you can
Ride the BUS!

Fed up with driving?

Want to read while you ride?

Sick of searching for a parking space?

Burdened by parking fees and traffic congestion?

Is your patience on the highway running out of gas?

Join the thousands who choose the smart ride every day—

the public-transit bus.

Whether you're going to work, to school, or out for fun,

the city bus can get you there without hassles or headaches

for only $1.

1. What emotional words are used in this portion of the brochure?

_____

_____

_____

_____

_____

2. How is this picture used as a tool for persuasion?

_____

_____

_____

_____

_____

Inside Spread

WHY RIDE?

Besides ensuring your own safety and peace of mind, riding the bus can also benefit your wallet and the environment.

- *You can save up to two hundred gallons of gasoline a year commuting by bus.*
- *Riding the bus for one year can prevent 9.1 pounds of hydrocarbons from polluting the air.*

While riding, you can read the newspaper, use your laptop computer, do homework, or just enjoy the scenery. More and more people are riding the bus, so why shouldn't you? Take advantage of this opportunity before the bus passes you by.

WHERE CAN I GO?

The transit bus provides service to educational facilities, downtown businesses, surrounding suburbs, and numerous shopping centers. Buses run an average of every ten minutes during peak commuting hours.

Middle Panel

STILL NOT CONVINCED?

Check out some comments from the latest rider survey.

"I used to drive my car, but I got tired of the traffic and stress. Now I ride the bus every day and arrive to work relaxed and ready to start my day."—Angie H.

"I started riding the bus three months ago, and it has really made a difference in my budget." —Jeanne W.

"The buses are always punctual and clean." —Joe P.

Back Panel

JOIN THE RANKS OF RIDERS TODAY.

For the nearest routes and schedules, call 1-800-BUS-RIDE.

Wheatland Public Transit System

Central offices located at 1206 Twin Oaks, Wheatland, WY 00001-0001

---

3. How are the facts on the inside spread used to persuade the reader?

_____

_____

_____

_____

4. Is the bandwagon technique used in the inside spread? Where?

_____

_____

_____

_____

_____

5. How are these rider quotations a form of persuasion?

_____

_____

_____

_____

_____

for **CHAPTER 8** | page 296 | *continued*   **TEST**

DIRECTIONS Use the information from the brochure you have just read to complete the graphic organizer.

Identifying Persuasive Techniques

▶ PERSUASIVE TECHNIQUE	▶ EXAMPLE FROM BROCHURE	▶ EXPLANATION OF PURPOSE
	More and more people are riding the bus, so why shouldn't you?	
		These words are used to create negative feelings in the readers toward driving a car instead of riding a bus.
Testimonial		

Writing Workshop: Persuasive Brochure

DIRECTIONS Use the following guidelines to help you revise and correct the brochure on the next page.

THE FRONT PANEL SHOULD

- open with a catchy slogan
- identify the product, service, or cause and its intended audience

THE INSIDE SPREAD SHOULD

- sell the primary idea with facts, examples, and statistics
- include section headings or subheadings
- use graphics to emphasize major points visually

THE MIDDLE PANEL SHOULD

- continue drawing the reader's attention
- use additional eye-catching graphics
- provide information

THE BACK PANEL SHOULD

- provide necessary contact information
- tell the reader what action to take

REMEMBER TO

- ❏ eliminate clichés
- ❏ maintain a consistent verb tense

Writing Workshop: Revising and Proofreading

DIRECTIONS The following persuasive brochure was written in response to this prompt:

Make a brochure to support a school-sponsored organization.

The brochure contains problems in content, style, and grammar.

- Use the space in the margins to revise the brochure and correct the errors.
- If you cannot fit some of your revisions on these pages, rewrite the revised sections on a separate piece of paper.

Front Panel

a. Problem with slogan

Project Sprout

Support

Wellsbrook High School's efforts to transform a vacant lot into a beautiful, outdoor learning space.

Project Sprout is a plan that creates an outdoor garden classroom and extended learning beyond the walls of the school.

b. Problem with verb tense

Inside Panel

c. Problem with missing heading

The project provides the students and surrounding community with the opportunity to cultivate plants, learn about the environment, and appreciate nature.

HOW WILL THIS HELP OUR STUDENTS?

Students can become more involved in their education if we put our money where our mouth is and create an outdoor classroom. Research has shown that effective environmental education is rooted in a problem-solving, action-oriented, and hands-on approach. Students will reap the benefits of developing problem-solving skills as well as critical- and creative-thinking skills.

d. Problem with clichés

Middle Panel

Back Panel

e. Problem with clichés

WHO WILL USE THE OUTDOOR CLASSROOM?

Believe it or not, the Project Sprout classroom will be open to all members of Wellsbrook High School, their families, and members of the community. Other secondary and elementary schools in the area will also be invited to use the outdoor classroom.

COME REAP WHAT YOU SOW, AND HELP PROJECT SPROUT GROW.

To GET INVOLVED today, contact the Wellsbrook High School Ecology Club sponsor, Mr. Jones, at 475-9786.

Also, come to the Project Sprout meetings in the school library every Wednesday at 7:00 p.m.

Let's face it, this project is too good to pass up.

Writing Complete Sentences

REVISING PHRASE FRAGMENTS

DIRECTIONS   Create a complete sentence from each of the following phrase fragments. Make your corrections between the lines. Add capitalization and punctuation wherever necessary.

        Ellen
Example   has been a gymnast⊙
      ∧

1. in the park

2. managing the store

3. motivated and energized

4. a classic car

5. to school

REVISING SUBORDINATE CLAUSE FRAGMENTS

DIRECTIONS   Create a complete sentence from each of the following subordinate clauses.

- Add an independent clause at the beginning or end of the subordinate clause.
- Add capitalization and punctuation wherever necessary.

        Josh won a music scholarship
Example   because he has a beautiful voice⊙
      ∧

6. before I returned to the laboratory

7. who is always fun to be around

8. that was made by Albert's sister

9. when he finished reading the book

10. which the meteorologists had predicted

REVISING RUN-ON SENTENCES

DIRECTIONS The following items are confusing because they are run-on sentences. Using the method of revision indicated in parentheses, correct each run-on sentence. Make your corrections between the lines. Add capitalization and punctuation wherever necessary.

Example 1. We could not afford the new sports utility vehicle we bought ^; *consequently,* ^
                the used truck. (Use a semicolon and a conjunctive adverb.)

11. Much of central Texas is filled with green, rolling hills people commonly refer to it as the

Hill Country. (Use a semicolon and a conjunctive adverb.)

12. Her first piano recital was a complete success, she played better than I have ever heard her

play before. (Make into two sentences.)

13. I prefer renting movies to watching regular television there are too many commercials on

television. (Use a semicolon.)

14. Yori did not win the track meet he trained hard for it. (Use a comma and a coordinating

conjunction.)

15. Ruben wants to buy a new computer he needs to shop around for one that is reasonably

priced. (Use a semicolon and a conjunctive adverb.)

16. Mom loves to shop at flea markets she's an expert at finding valuable antiques at bargain-

basement prices. (Use a comma and a coordinating conjunction.)

17. It was snowing outside they decided to take the bus. (Use a semicolon.)

18. We are studying the history of classical music our teacher, Mr. Schultz, is particularly fond

of late eighteenth-century music. (Make into two sentences.)

19. We used to see deer all the time in that field recent construction has driven them away.

(Use a comma and a coordinating conjunction.)

20. Jeremiah and I could not go to the football game on Friday night we went to the park and

jogged. (Use a semicolon and a conjunctive adverb.)

REVISING FRAGMENTS AND RUN-ON SENTENCES

DIRECTIONS The following passage contains several sentences that need to be improved. Rewrite the passage correctly, making your revisions in the space between the lines. Change the punctuation and capitalization wherever necessary.

Look for
- sentence fragments
- run-on sentences

Example   Karly *enjoys* all kinds of sports.

Working Out

My cousin Karly. Who is a determined athlete. She takes tae kwon do three times each week, runs at least two miles every day and lifts weights. At the gym twice each week. Because of her busy schedule, we hardly ever see her Karly's diligence has taught all of us something about perseverance and discipline.

Karly started taking tae kwon do. A Korean martial art. When she was just six years old. She is now sixteen years old and has earned a fifth-degree black belt. The first time I ever watched her compete, I was astounded by three things. Her speed, her flexibility, and her concentration. These skills, she says, complement her other athletic pursuits, running and lifting weights.

Running may not seem like a difficult sport. Runners, however, do need flexibility and a certain amount of speed. Stretching helps keep Karly's muscles flexible. She has increased her speed while preparing for a marathon. That will be held next month. Even if she weren't preparing for a marathon, Karly says that running at a fast pace provides a better aerobic workout than running at a slow pace Karly's cardiovascular fitness gives her lots of energy.

Writing Effective Sentences

COMBINING SENTENCES

DIRECTIONS Using all of the sentence-combining skills you have learned, revise and rewrite each of the following sets of sentences into one sentence. You may combine by

- inserting words or phrases
- creating compound subjects and verbs or compound sentences
- creating complex sentences

You may have to add or delete some words. Add punctuation where necessary. Mark your revisions between the lines.

Example **1.** Kaylee Mendez will introduce the guest speaker to the student

,̂ an engineer from NASA,̂

assembler. ~~The guest speaker is an engineer from NASA~~*e*.

1. Thomas Paine was famous. Thomas Paine was a writer.

2. Kalil runs five miles every day. Kalil is training for an upcoming meet.

3. Winters in most of Texas are pleasantly mild. Summers in most of Texas can be uncomfortably

hot.

4. You will see the cabin. You pass the large pine tree.

5. I left my books. My books are at Nancy's house.

6. *Romeo and Juliet* is the story of two star-crossed lovers. *Romeo and Juliet* is a drama written

by William Shakespeare.

7. Jupiter is the largest planet in the solar system. Jupiter rotates faster than any planet we know.

8. Our school hosted a fund-raiser for a local charity. The fund-raiser was a complete success.

9. Manuel sang ballads and told jokes for the spring show. Shelby sang ballads and told jokes for

the spring show.

10. Someone will drive the car. That person will test the new brakes.

IMPROVING SENTENCE STYLE

DIRECTIONS Using what you have learned about improving sentence style, revise each of the following items. Remember to add correct capitalization and punctuation. Use the headings above each set of sentences to guide you. Make your corrections between the lines.

Example *Varying Sentence Beginnings:*

> *Because we*
> **12.** ~~We~~ worked until 3:00 A.M. ~~and~~ ⌃*we* got the project done.

Using Parallel Structure

11. There is much to do at Yellowstone National Park, including hiking, fishing, and to camp.

12. Andrea is a counselor who has patience, can understand her clients, and dedication.

Revising Stringy Sentences

13. I got into the habit of reading the daily newspaper last year to find out what was happening in the presidential race and what I discovered was a lot more than what I had expected and there was a lot going on in my city, the state and country, and around the world that I didn't know about.

14. Sarah used to watch television for hours, and we could not get her off the couch, but now she hardly watches the television at all because she has found a new passion—aerobics!

Revising Wordy Sentences

15. Rosa has been a computer analyst, and she is a highly skilled analyst.

16. The motivations that led me to join a karate class are varied and include a desire to learn about its philosophy, to learn self-defense, and to get exercise.

Varying Sentence Beginnings

17. Grandma made a big breakfast before anyone even knew what time it was.

18. My parents were baffled and wanted to know why I had decided to take music lessons.

Varying Sentence Structure

19. Some people love cats. Other people prefer dogs.

20. Martin will go to the beach if his sister wants to go. He will not go if she

does not want to go.

REVISING A PARAGRAPH
DIRECTIONS   Using what you have learned about combining sentences and
improving sentence style, revise the following paragraph to make it
smoother and more varied. Combining different kinds of sentences will
make the paragraph much easier to read. Make your corrections in the space
between the lines.

                              Because
Example   Alexander the Great was a brilliant military strategist. ̶H̶e won
                 ʌ

many battles.

The Great Conqueror

Alexander the Great lived from 356 to 323 B.C. He began his military career

while still in his teens. His father, Philip II, was killed. Alexander was twenty

years old. He became king of the Macedonians. His marches through Greece

and Asia Minor were successful. They proved that Alexander was an ambi-

tious king. They also proved that he was a skilled military tactician. The

Egyptians were glad to see him and tired of the heavy-handed Persians that

ruled Egypt, so the Egyptians crowned Alexander pharaoh in 331 B.C., and his

defeat of the Persians in the Battle of Gaugamela in that same year ended

more than two hundred years of Persian rule in southwest Asia.

for **CHAPTER 11** | *page 370*

CHAPTER TEST

Understanding Paragraphs and Compositions

DIRECTIONS Read the paragraphs below. Then, use what you have learned about paragraphs to answer the questions in the right column.

Paragraph 1

Whether you are trying to build muscle mass or simply tone your muscles, your form—how you hold or position your body—when training with weights is important. Good form can help you target a muscle or muscle group as well as help you avoid injury. For example, if you wanted to tone or build the muscles in your upper arm, you could use small, hand-held weights, commonly referred to as dumbbells. Most gyms have dumbbells. What does this have to do with form? Well, your upper arm has two main muscles: the *bicep*, in the front, and the *tricep*, in the back. If you pull the dumbbell up towards your shoulder, you will tone or build the bicep. If you push the dumbbell out behind you, you will tone or build the tricep. The different movements target the specified muscle, but beware: Moving the wrong way or holding your body in the wrong position can cause serious injury.

Paragraph 2

The American robin is an appealing species partly because of its appearance and partly because it seems to be the ideal family bird. Robins are well known for their distinct reddish orange breasts. As with many species of birds, it is the male robin that has the brighter, more distinct markings. The female robin, who lays the beautiful greenish blue eggs, can lay up to fifteen eggs in a given year—not at the same time, however. Robins typically raise two broods a year. Both parents feed the babies after they have hatched. The young robins are ready to leave the nest in just fifteen days. While the female robin incubates her second clutch, the young from the first brood join the adult males in communal nocturnal roosts. When the young of the second brood are old enough, all the robins move to the communal roost.

PARAGRAPH 1

1. Underline the topic sentence.

2. Circle the clincher sentence.

3. Cross out the sentence that does not support the main idea.

4. What kind of supporting details are used in this paragraph—sensory details, facts, statistics, examples, anecdotes?

   _____

5. What is the organization pattern of this paragraph—chronological, spatial, logical, order of importance?

   _____

PARAGRAPH 2

6. What is the main idea?

   _____

   _____

7. What is the organization pattern of this paragraph—chronological, spatial, logical, order of importance?

   _____

8. Circle the transitional words and direct references.

DIRECTIONS Read the following paragraphs. The one body paragraph is taken from the composition. Answer the questions in the right column.

Introductory Paragraph

Since the late 1700s, Great Britain has witnessed a constantly changing world. The American and French Revolutions encouraged democratic idealists to work for social and political reforms. During Queen Victoria's rule, the nation gained strength as a major industrial power. Then the mechanical death and destruction of the two world wars of the twentieth century shook the habits and beliefs of the country. The British literature of the past two hundred years reflects the social and political changes of each era; it can be divided into three major literary periods.

The first of these, the Romantic Age, produced literature that emphasizes imagination, intuition, the importance of the individual, and personal expression. The literature of the second period, the Victorian Age, pinpoints how scientific discoveries and advancements, as well as industrialization, often clashed with social conventions. Modern Age literature often emphasizes the alienation of the individual, pessimism, and stoicism.

Body Paragraph

Unlike literature in the Romantic Age, which focused mainly on the individual, literature of the Victorian Age focused on how people dealt with drastic scientific and industrial changes. Several scientific discoveries in the fields of geology, astronomy, and biology shook the basic foundation of Victorian culture. People stood between the past that they understood and a future of unknown possibilities. People wanted to learn more and, at the same time, were afraid of what changes new knowledge would bring. The work of one Victorian poet illustrates this conflict. In _Idylls of the King,_ Alfred, Lord Tennyson portrays a desire to return to the values of the past. In contrast, his "Ulysses," portrays a desire to press forward, to learn all there is to learn, even if doing so seems frightening and unsure.

Concluding Paragraph

Each period of British literature reflects the concerns of its people. The Romantics look inward; the Victorians look to the future with hope and fear; twentieth-century writers look around them at a world full of misery and suffering. For two hundred years, political, social, and cultural changes shaped the literature of a nation.

INTRODUCTION

9. Underline the thesis statement.

10. Which of these techniques does the writer use—question, anecdote or example, startling fact or unusual opinion, background information?

_____

11. When you exclude the thesis statement, does the introduction move from the general to the specific or vice versa?

_____

BODY

12. What is the main idea of this paragraph?

13. Circle the direct references and transitional expressions.

14. What kinds of details are used to support the thesis—sensory details, facts, statistics, examples, anecdotes?

_____

_____

CONCLUSION

15. Which of the following techniques is used—restatement, reference to the introduction, personal reaction, quotation, summary?

_____

DIRECTIONS Use the sentences below to write an introductory paragraph and two to four body paragraphs for a short informative composition about naval warships. You do not have to use all the information, but use as much as you need to develop your paragraphs fully.

- Begin by developing a thesis statement. (*Helpful hint:* The United States has six different types of warships.)
- Next, write the introduction.
- Then, develop a series of short body paragraphs that support your thesis statement.
- Finally, evaluate and revise your paragraphs to make sure that they demonstrate unity, coherence, and elaboration. Be sure to use transitional expressions and direct references.

– United States warships are designed for combat.

– An aircraft carrier is one type of warship.

– The main purpose of an aircraft carrier is to carry bomber and fighter planes to their destination.

– Aircraft carriers can also carry antisubmarine aircraft and helicopters and can house a crew of six thousand.

– A cruiser is a kind of warship.

– Cruisers are heavily armed with missiles, rockets, and torpedoes, but the ships themselves are small, only about six hundred feet long.

– A cruiser accompanies and defends aircraft carriers.

– The amphibious warfare ship is a warship.

– An amphibious warfare ship is extremely versatile, and it looks like a miniature aircraft carrier.

– Amphibious warfare ships are slightly larger than cruisers, measuring about eight hundred feet.

– The amphibious warfare ship does not have the equipment necessary to launch or land planes.

– Amphibious warfare ships can carry troops, weapons, and other vehicles, such as amphibious tractors and landing craft.

– A single amphibious warfare ship can carry as many as twenty to thirty helicopters.

– Destroyers also have a variety of uses.

– Destroyers can be as short as 375 feet or as long as 560 feet.

– Destroyers can attack enemy shores. They can perform oceanic search-and-rescue operations.

– Destroyers can defend other warships.

Parts of Speech Overview: Identification and Function

A. IDENTIFYING TYPES OF NOUNS AND PRONOUNS Each of the following sentences is followed by the names of one kind of noun and one kind of pronoun in parentheses. In each sentence, underline each of that kind of noun once and each of that kind of pronoun twice.

Example 1. Be thankful for the <u>freedom</u> and <u>opportunity</u> <u><u>that</u></u> we have in the United States to elect our representatives. (*abstract noun, relative pronoun*)

1. Everyone suspects that Miss Hendrick herself will direct the production of *Our Town*. (*compound noun, intensive pronoun*)

2. "The music box you sent for my birthday fills me with happiness each time I play it," Joan wrote to her aunt. (*abstract noun, personal pronoun*)

3. Who said that they should keep the store open every day in November? (*common noun, interrogative pronoun*)

4. Last weekend at Lost Valley State Park, I saw Robert and his family, who were there hiking. (*proper noun, relative pronoun*)

5. Yes, somebody should meet Eddie at the station, but does anyone know when his train arrives? (*concrete noun, indefinite pronoun*)

6. When the band played that song, which I like a lot, the audience went wild. (*collective noun, relative pronoun*)

7. These are certainly beautiful shirts and coats, but I don't need any new clothes. (*common noun, demonstrative pronoun*)

8. Both of the twins learned about Hinduism from their new book on India. (*abstract noun, indefinite pronoun*)

9. That was not a straight kick, and now the football has landed in her garden. (*compound noun, demonstrative pronoun*)

10. Frank asked himself why he waited until Wednesday to start his report on the French Revolution. (*proper noun, reflexive pronoun*)

B. IDENTIFYING VERBS AND VERB PHRASES Underline the verb or verb phrase in each of the following sentences. For each verb phrase, circle all helping verbs.

Example 1. I (have) heard different theories about early explorers in the Americas.

11. Professor Mike Xu is receiving attention for an interesting theory.

12. Have you read reports of the Texas Christian University faculty member's ideas?

13. According to Xu, the ancient Chinese may have arrived in the New World first.

14. The Chinese could have crossed the Pacific Ocean more than 3,000 years ago.

15. Does that surprise you?

16. Some symbols from the Olmec, an early civilization in the Americas, and from the Shang

dynasty in China look remarkably alike.

17. Xu has based his theory on these similarities between ancient Olmec and Chinese symbols.

18. We will likely hear more about Xu's theory.

19. Scholars around the world are giving serious attention to Xu's work.

20. Numerous authoritative publications and news agencies have covered Xu's theories.

C. IDENTIFYING TYPES OF VERBS Each of the following sentences is followed by the names of two
kinds of verbs in parentheses. Circle the name of the kind of verb or verb phrase that is italicized in the
sentence.

Example 1. The girls *remained* motionless as the skunk passed them. (*action verb* or

(*linking verb*))

21. *Do* you *think* that the governor will open the fair this year? (*action verb* or *linking verb*)

22. The audience *waited* quietly for the show to start. (*transitive verb* or *intransitive verb*)

23. This *has been* a marvelous day! (*action verb* or *linking verb*)

24. Ray *bought* a box of crackers, a wedge of cheese, and a bottle of water. (*transitive verb* or

intransitive verb)

25. The curious cat *stared* at the motionless mechanical toy for a long time. (*transitive verb* or

intransitive verb)

26. "Make sure that you *answer* the questions in the order they are given," Mr. Lopez said. (*action*

verb or *linking verb*)

27. When she finished her homework, Iva *sent* two e-mails to friends. (*transitive verb* or *intransitive*

verb)

28. The wind *grew* stronger as the storm approached. (*action verb* or *linking verb*)

29. The marathon *will end* here about five hours from now. (*transitive verb* or *intransitive verb*)

30. "The Thai stir-fry *tastes* great!" Loretta said. (*action verb* or *linking verb*)

D. IDENTIFYING ADJECTIVES, ADVERBS, PREPOSITIONS, CONJUNCTIONS, AND INTERJECTIONS Each of the following sentences contains several italicized words and word groups. Above each italicized word or word group, identify its part of speech. Use the following abbreviations: *ADJ* for *adjective*, *ADV* for *adverb*, *PREP* for *preposition*, *CONJ* for *conjunction*, *INT* for *interjection*.

Example 1. The *party* decorations were *particularly beautiful* and pleased *not only* the young
            ADJ   ADV   ADJ   CONJ
           CONJ
           guests *but also* their parents.

31. Our *lunch* bell *usually* rings *at* eleven o'clock, *but* I didn't hear it today.

32. "*Wow*! That dog is *really clever*!" Martha exclaimed.

33. *Both* the compass *and* the binoculars were gifts *from* Uncle Fred.

34. We had, *oh*, maybe *thirty* relatives *here* for *a* tasty potluck.

35. *After* hearing *those* words of encouragement, Meg's mood became *much brighter*.

36. My *older* brother won a *silver* medal at the interscholastic track meet *yesterday*.

37. *According to* Ms. Sanders, the council *never* will approve the *freeway* plan.

38. I *sincerely* hope it snows *during* the next few days, *yet* I know the chances aren't *good*.

39. *The* new museum exhibit will *especially* appeal *to* people interested in *Old World* culture.

40. *Which* color *best* matches *this* curtain that will go *above* the front windows?

E. IDENTIFYING PARTS OF SPEECH Above each italicized word in the following sentences, identify the part of speech of that word. Use the following abbreviations: *N* for *noun*, *PRO* for *pronoun*, *V* for *verb*, *ADJ* for *adjective*, *ADV* for *adverb*, *PREP* for *preposition*, and *CONJ* for *conjunction*.

Example 1. Since the storm sounds *near*, we'd better go inside.
                             ADV

41. *This* map is easier to read than that one.

42. "*This* looks like a winning play to me!" the coach yelled.

43. The first *stop* on the tour will be the McGregor Home.

44. "Please *stop* asking me when we'll get there," Dad said.

45. Have you ever driven across the *Oklahoma* panhandle?

46. Will Rogers was very proud of being from *Oklahoma*.

47. Let's go *inside* and see what's happening!

48. The duck stayed *inside* the barn until the dogs ran away.

49. "Everyone *but* me gets to go to the show," Sam complained.

50. We had hoped to move to a bigger apartment, *but* now we must wait.

The Parts of a Sentence: Subjects, Predicates, Complements

A. IDENTIFYING SENTENCES Identify each of the following groups of words as a sentence or a sentence fragment. On the line provided, write *S* for *sentence* or *F* for *fragment*.

Examples   _F_   **1.** Moving to a new apartment.

     _S_   **2.** Jason's family moved to a new apartment.

_____ **1.** Lived in an apartment on the second floor for five years.

_____ **2.** When a larger apartment with more bedrooms became available.

_____ **3.** Jason, his sister, and his mother were excited about the move.

_____ **4.** A separate room for each of them for the first time.

_____ **5.** Packing was a big job.

_____ **6.** Since they had collected boxes from neighborhood stores.

_____ **7.** Used crumpled newspapers to put around breakable items.

_____ **8.** Friends helped them make the seven-block move.

_____ **9.** Have you ever moved from one home to another?

_____ **10.** Then you know it can be quite an experience.

B. IDENTIFYING SUBJECTS AND PREDICATES In each of the following sentences, underline the complete subject once and the complete predicate twice. Then, circle each simple subject and each simple predicate. A simple subject or a simple predicate may be compound.

Example 1. The rowdy (team) and the (coaches) (celebrated) their victory.

11. The telephone call woke me from a sound sleep late last night.

12. Were those books and records on sale after the holidays?

13. Scoring with a long field goal in the final seconds of last Saturday's game, our junior varsity team won.

14. There are the chemicals for this morning's science project.

15. Tom Hanks, my favorite actor, has starred in many fine movies.

16. The powerful tigress with her cubs walked in a stately manner across the grass.

17. Do you know the names of any famous Scottish authors?

18. Maria's beautiful sapphire had been cut in a star-shaped pattern.

19. The parade on St. Patrick's Day probably will last five hours.

20. The three brothers must wait for their father to return before leaving the house.

21. Before the test, we studied the rules and practiced the problems.

22. One of the papers was thrown into the hedge.

23. How many gold medals did Wilma Rudolph win?

24. By the gate near the house wait the boy and his dog.

25. During the summer, temperatures along the Rio Grande can be extremely hot.

26. All of the deer in the small herd and the other animals nearby stopped and listened.

27. Organic fruits and vegetables have been grown and sold here for a decade.

28. Here is your sandwich for lunch.

29. Where were the boys and girls from Mr. Rowse's class?

30. After washing the clothes, we vacuumed the living room and cleaned the windows.

C. IDENTIFYING COMPLEMENTS Identify the kind of complement that is italicized in each of the
following sentences. Above each italicized complement, write *DO* for *direct object*, *IO* for *indirect object*,
PN for *predicate nominative*, or *PA* for *predicate adjective*.

> **Example 1.** Do you know *what we should do*? — with DO written above

31. After she arrived, Grace remained *quiet* and *thoughtful*.

32. I have already worn *it* three times this week.

33. What a good *example* that is!

34. We took our *dog* and *cat* to the vet last week for grooming.

35. Someone sent *her* a new sweater, but I don't know who.

36. How *funny* that costume looked!

37. My little sister wrote a clever *poem* about her first camping trip.

38. The soup's main ingredients are *water*, *tomatoes*, and *garlic*.

39. Daniel told *Lynn* and *me* the secret about the ring.

40. When did the original thirteen colonies officially become the *United States of America*?

D. CLASSIFYING AND PUNCTUATING SENTENCES Classify each of the following sentences by writing
DEC for *declarative*, *IMP* for *imperative*, *INT* for *interrogative*, or *EXC* for *exclamatory* on the line provided.
Add the correct end punctuation to each sentence.

> **Example** *IMP* **1.** Please tell us about the famous American Indian, Sequoya.

_____ **41.** Sequoya was a Cherokee who lived from around 1760 to 1843

_____ **42.** Did you know that he invented a system of writing

_____ **43.** Wow, that's a major achievement

_____ **44.** It took Sequoya twelve years to complete his writing system

_____ **45.** Look at these pictures of Sequoya and his symbols for written communication

_____ **46.** Weren't a number of books and newspapers published for Cherokee readers

_____ **47.** Yes, thousands of Cherokee read and wrote the language

_____ **48.** Is it true that Sequoya represented American Indian peoples in Washington, D.C.

_____ **49.** Remember that Sequoya helped many people in many ways

_____ **50.** What a remarkable person he was

The Phrase: Prepositional, Verbal, and Appositive Phrases

A. IDENTIFYING PREPOSITIONAL PHRASES AND THE WORDS THEY MODIFY In each of the following sentences, underline each prepositional phrase and draw an arrow to the word it modifies.

Example 1. After the film about Italy, we discussed Italian culture for an hour or so.

1. That can of white paint will be used as a primer at the new house.

2. Before last Monday, the girls had never snorkeled beyond the cove.

3. The squirrel scampered under the stones in front of the back fence.

4. Paul's sister reads amazingly well for a four-year-old.

5. Everyone in our family was sick with the flu, but we are all well now.

6. The group behind us said that they had particularly enjoyed traveling aboard a historic train along the Mississippi River.

7. Howard became exhausted from too much activity.

8. Toward evening, the shadows upon the sidewalk lengthen.

9. The glass beside the pitcher on the counter is the one for Emily.

10. The team beat its rival by only two points.

B. IDENTIFYING VERBALS Underline the participle, the gerund, or the infinitive in each of the following sentences. Then, identify it by writing *PART* for *participle*, *GER* for *gerund*, or *INF* for *infinitive* on the line provided.

Example _PART_ **1.** The boys fell asleep in the rocking boat.

_____ **11.** Walking is considered one of the best exercises, so I walk a mile every day.

_____ **12.** To her credit, Mrs. Kelly has always been quick to praise those who did the best that they could.

_____ **13.** Professionals removed the fallen tree from the driveway.

_____ **14.** Darren has given juggling his full attention.

_____ **15.** Would you like some roasted garlic with your meal?

_____ **16.** I have been noticing how many people enjoy surfing the Web.

_____ **17.** Although she has many talents, Janey's main goal is to write.

_____ **18.** Shouting, the fans eagerly rushed onto the field.

_____ **19.** Before eating, Andy always washes his hands.

_____ **20.** "Who knows which one to believe?" Wyatt asked.

C. **IDENTIFYING VERBAL PHRASES** Identify which kind of verbal phrase is italicized in each of the following sentences. On the line provided, write *PART* for *participial phrase*, *GER* for *gerund phrase*, or *INF* for *infinitive phrase*.

Example ___*INF*___ **1.** *To find facts for her report about her hometown of El Paso, Texas,* Carmen went to the library.

_____ **21.** *Researching El Paso* turned out to be enjoyable as well as informative for Carmen.

_____ **22.** She began by *learning about early inhabitants of the area, the Manso and Suma peoples.*

_____ **23.** *Claiming the land for Spain in 1598,* Juan de Oñate secured the area for Spanish settlers.

_____ **24.** The Church in Spain sent priests and missionaries *to establish missions and found settlements.*

_____ **25.** Carmen was surprised *to discover that the area contained the first two towns in Texas.*

_____ **26.** Carmen's home, *built by Spanish settlers almost two centuries ago* has been in her family for generations.

_____ **27.** She and her family enjoy *visiting one of her aunts in Juarez, El Paso's sister city in Mexico.*

_____ **28.** Carmen decided *to include in her report two pictures of United States and Mexican railroads in El Paso during the 1880s.*

_____ **29.** Carmen's great-grandmother had many tales *to tell about the exploits of Pancho Villa and about the growth of El Paso in the early 1900s.*

_____ **30.** *Having gathered so much information of all kinds for her report,* Carmen has decided to make a multimedia presentation.

D. **IDENTIFYING APPOSITIVES AND APPOSITIVE PHRASES** Underline the appositive or appositive phrase in each of the following sentences.

Example 1. A joyful and clever child, Sue Ellen is a pleasure to baby-sit.

31. Our neighbor Ms. Garza is a computer engineer.

32. Mount Rainier, a 14,410-foot-tall colossus, is in the Cascade Range.

33. That magazine, the most popular new publication in the library, was started two years ago.

34. A dependable and trusted employee, Dan was promoted to a supervisory position.

35. The Nelsons' canary, Pete, is smarter than most birds, I think.

36. Candice bought a new winter coat, one with a hood.

37. Was my cousin Nick invited to the party?

38. His table, a masterpiece of inlaid wood, is on display at the gallery.

39. The Russian space station Mir has been in orbit since 1986.

40. Dad's business partner is originally from Argentina, a large and varied country in the southern

tip of South America.

E. IDENTIFYING PHRASES   For each of the following sentences, identify the kind of phrase that is
italicized. On the line provided, write *PREP* for *prepositional phrase*, *PART* for *participial phrase*, *GER* for
gerund phrase, *INF* for *infinitive phrase*, or *APP* for *appositive phrase*.

Example _PREP_   **1.** *By memorizing the rules and learning how to apply them*, Jan advanced rapidly.

_____ **41.** The lawn mower was fairly easy *to assemble in only an hour or so*.

_____ **42.** Kate Greenaway, *an English painter and illustrator*, is one of my favorite artists.

_____ **43.** We hid the presents *underneath the back stairs*, but Jon found them.

_____ **44.** *Studying for at least an hour each night*, Randy worked hard to make good grades.

_____ **45.** After they get home from school, the twins like *riding their bicycles and playing chase*.

_____ **46.** *Creating crossword puzzles* would be a challenging job that I think I would enjoy.

_____ **47.** "From now on, you can take your new binoculars *to football games and other sports events*

so that you can get a closer look at the action," Dad said.

_____ **48.** *A mixture of camomile and other herbs*, the tea is very soothing.

_____ **49.** The movie *filmed in our town last year* opens tomorrow nationwide.

_____ **50.** Max's decision *to run for president* was a surprise.

The Clause: Independent Clauses and Subordinate Clauses

A. IDENTIFYING INDEPENDENT AND SUBORDINATE CLAUSES For each of the following sentences, identify the clause in italics as independent or subordinate. On the line provided, write *IND* for *independent* or *SUB* for *subordinate*.

Example ___*SUB*___ **1.** Did you know *that the ancestors of most African Americans came from one area of Africa?*

_____ **1.** I have used reliable resources; *therefore, my facts should be correct.*

_____ **2.** The area, *which was about the size of the continental United States*, was known as the Western Sudan.

_____ **3.** I found a map *that shows its various borders, including the Atlantic Ocean and the Sahara.*

_____ **4.** The Western Sudan was a seat of power *because it was not only large but also had many valuable resources.*

_____ **5.** *The Western Sudan was ruled by three large empires* that lasted from the fourth century A.D. to almost 1600.

_____ **6.** *Ghana, Mali, and Songhai were the names of these empires*, which each made a special contribution to the development of the area and its inhabitants.

_____ **7.** *Since the Ghanians were the first people in western Africa to smelt iron ore and use it to make weapons*, they were able to build an empire by conquering surrounding nations.

_____ **8.** Almost one thousand years later, the Mali empire took control of Ghana, but *Mali rule lasted only a couple of hundred years.*

_____ **9.** *Although the Songhai Empire was equally short-lived*, it carried on the advancement of learning and culture that had blossomed in Mali.

_____ **10.** *The Western Sudan lost its position of power* when Morocco conquered Songhai in 1591.

B. CLASSIFYING SUBORDINATE CLAUSES On the line provided, identify the kind of subordinate clause that is italicized. Write *ADJ* for *adjective clause*, *ADV* for *adverb clause*, or *N* for *noun clause*. For each adjective or adverb clause, circle the word or words that the clause modifies. Above each noun clause, identify how the noun clause is used. Write *S* for *subject*, *PN* for *predicate nominative*, *DO* for *direct object*, *IO* for *indirect object*, or *OP* for *object of the preposition*.

Example ___*N*___ **1.** Someone should give *whoever invented the remote control* a medal. (*IO*)

_____ **11.** *If you want to go to the farm*, you'll have to leave early tomorrow morning.

_____ **12.** "This is the movie *that I told you about*," Jerome said.

_____ **13.** The champion will be *whoever spells the last two words correctly.*

_____ **14.** Billy is not someone *who can be easily fooled.*

_____ **15.** Please turn the volume down on the radio *so that I can listen for the doorbell.*

_____ **16.** *While the sun is shining,* we should turn around and start heading back to shore.

_____ **17.** *Just as they walked into the room,* the clock stopped.

_____ **18.** The Japanese economy is a subject *about which much has been written.*

_____ **19.** Mrs. Lloyd did not say *when she will give the test papers back.*

_____ **20.** *Why the water was turned off* is a mystery.

C. **IDENTIFYING AND CLASSIFYING SUBORDINATE CLAUSES** Underline the subordinate clause in each of the following sentences. Then, on the line provided, classify each subordinate clause by writing *ADJ* for *adjective clause, ADV* for *adverb clause,* or *N* for *noun clause.*

Example __*ADJ*__ **1.** I saw a painting at the gallery of someone who looks just like you.

_____ **21.** Who knows what toys will be popular next year?

_____ **22.** Beth, whose opinion I value, is out of town unfortunately.

_____ **23.** "Be sure to leave the faucet dripping so that the water pipes won't freeze tonight,"

Ms. New said.

_____ **24.** My brothers and I help others whenever we can.

_____ **25.** As soon as Robyn gets new glasses, she will be allowed to drive the car again.

_____ **26.** He is the one whom I like the best.

_____ **27.** What the classroom really needs is better lighting.

_____ **28.** This station, which I found by accident, plays all the latest hits.

_____ **29.** Because the auditorium is being repainted, the assembly will be in the gym.

_____ **30.** Monday also is when the library is open later in the evening.

_____ **31.** Al and Debbie renewed their fishing licenses at the same time they rented the boat.

_____ **32.** Unless you stop arguing, I won't go with you.

_____ **33.** It's always nice to talk to that receptionist who is cheerful on the telephone.

_____ **34.** Strawberries and peaches are two kinds of fruit that taste best only in season.

_____ **35.** You should tell her that we're leaving now, don't you think?

_____ **36.** If the newspaper rack is empty, try the newsstand.

_____ **37.** Even with her hand injury, Janet can play the piano as well as she ever could.

_____ **38.** Most of the work will be done by whoever is on the day shift.

_____ **39.** Even though Rick is the oldest, he may not be the most qualified.

_____ **40.** Is that the boy whose father won the drawing for a new car?

D. CLASSIFYING SENTENCES ACCORDING TO STRUCTURE On the line provided, classify each sentence according to structure. Write *S* for *simple sentence*, *CD* for *compound sentence*, *CX* for *complex sentence*, or *CD-CX* for *compound-complex sentence*.

Example *CD-CX* **1.** Until we read the magazine article, we hadn't known about that new solar-powered car, nor had we heard about how efficient the new electric cars are.

_____ **41.** The store is usually open by now, but the owners may be on vacation, or maybe they're just late today.

_____ **42.** Both of our dogs, Joshua and Amy, ran behind the truck and barked loudly.

_____ **43.** The saxophonist played only two songs before he left the stage, and he never returned.

_____ **44.** For a change, Sean and Vivian ordered a la carte; however, they had to pay more than usual.

_____ **45.** The two Scouts folded the flag during the ceremony, and then they handed it to their den leader, and she, in turn, gave the flag to the pack leader.

_____ **46.** Wanting to help around the house, Bob cleaned his room and then organized all of the tools in the garage.

_____ **47.** Since they wanted to see the performers, Doris and Earl raced to the stage that had been set up in the center of the mall.

_____ **48.** After he ate, either Bruce watched TV or he took a nap.

_____ **49.** The math assignment I finished in study hall was similar to one that we had yesterday.

_____ **50.** The game postponed because of the rain has been rescheduled for tomorrow afternoon if the weather clears.

Agreement: Subject and Verb, Pronoun and Antecedent

A. IDENTIFYING VERBS THAT AGREE IN NUMBER WITH THEIR SUBJECTS In each of the following sentences, underline the correct form of the verb in parentheses.

Example 1. Picking apples from tops of trees (*look, looks*) like difficult work.

1. Nearly all of the fish in the aquarium usually (*swim, swims*) near the front.

2. Every photograph that we have had developed at those shops (*seem, seems*) too dark to me.

3. Seventy percent of the people who read the local paper every day, according to the poll, (*has, have*) a subscription to it.

4. Sioux Falls, the largest city in South Dakota, (*lie, lies*) along the Big Sioux River.

5. Evan, not any of the other team members, (*represent, represents*) the school at tournaments.

6. Alina and Helen (*plan, plans*) to work in the science lab after school.

7. Where (*is, are*) the snacks for the party?

8. Eight students in my American history class (*speak, speaks*) more than one language.

9. The egg rolls at my favorite Chinese restaurant (*contain, contains*) bamboo shoots.

10. (*Doesn't, Don't*) the program say that Shetland ponies are from a region of Scotland?

11. "The questions that most often (*trick, tricks*) me are about geography," Diane said.

12. Neither Elliott nor Robert (*work, works*) at the store anymore.

13. Molasses (*pours, pour*) out of a bottle very slowly.

14. Both of them (*has, have*) gotten better grades this semester.

15. Mr. Macy said that "Great African American Artists" (*is, are*) too broad a title for my report.

16. The chamber choir (*give, gives*) several performances a week at various club meetings and other events during the holiday season.

17. The puppy often (*lie, lies*) on the rug by the couch.

18. Each of the boys (*have, has*) American Indian ancestors, I'm told.

19. Blueberries (*is, are*) her favorite ingredient in the three-berry cobbler.

20. Either two cars or a truck (*is, are*) parked in their driveway all the time.

B. IDENTIFYING PRONOUNS AND ANTECEDENTS In each of the following sentences, underline the correct pronoun in parentheses. Then, circle the pronoun's antecedent.

Example 1. The faculty turned in (*its, their*) grades this afternoon.

21. Donna and Kim, who like (*her, their*) Spanish class, want to take French, too.

22. Fifty yards from shore might not seem far at all, but (*it, they*) felt like a mile as I swam to shore after I saw that shark's fin.

23. Neither of my skateboards will need to have (*its, their*) wheels replaced anytime soon.

24. *The Birds* is one of the most suspenseful films I've ever seen, but I don't recall who directed (*it, them*).

25. Many of the alumni recalled (*his or her, their*) childhoods in Harlem and Brooklyn.

26. My brother took economics in college and really enjoyed (*it, them*).

27. Did Ann or Lori leave (*her, their*) sunglasses lying on the table?

28. Both of the girls waited patiently in line with (*her, their*) aunt.

29. The club voted to keep (*its, their*) original bylaws.

30. Joanne and Bernadette wore (*her, their*) new track shoes to school.

C. PROOFREADING SENTENCES FOR SUBJECT-VERB AND PRONOUN-ANTECEDENT AGREEMENT Most
of the following sentences contain errors in agreement. Draw a line through each incorrect verb or pronoun, and write the correct form above it. If a sentence is already correct, write *C* on the line provided.

Example _____ **1.** Mario is one of those pianists who ~~plays his~~ *play their* best under pressure.

_____ **31.** Alice and Bev, who transferred to our school during the winter break, usually brings her lunches from home every day.

_____ **32.** The ranch families from the valley is having a barn raising for the new folks who bought the old Richardson place.

_____ **33.** Each of the boys who win today will receive their prize tomorrow.

_____ **34.** When the monsoons finally arrives, the rice paddies fill up quickly.

_____ **35.** To learn these dates is important for the test next week.

_____ **36.** The weather forecast said that Texas as well as most other Southern states are going to see drier weather than normal the next few months.

_____ **37.** The main ingredient in both casseroles is sweet potatoes.

_____ **38.** Becky, not any of her sisters, were the one who lost the ring.

_____ **39.** Apparently, those campers over there don't know how to build their fire correctly, and I think we should offer to help them.

_____ **40.** Many of the cast already knows nearly all of its lines.

_____ **41.** Before handling food, Mom always wash her hands with soap and warm water.

_____ **42.** The family usually agrees among one another when it take time to talk about things

that are important.

_____ **43.** Neither the beans nor the corn bread are ready yet.

_____ **44.** Here is the lettuce and tomatoes that Fay and Angelina need to make their tacos.

_____ **45.** Do Luis or Joey understand the assignment?

_____ **46.** John Steinbeck's *Of Mice and Men* have been made into a movie at least twice.

_____ **47.** Twenty dollars are a good price for four tickets; here's my share.

_____ **48.** Everyone on the girls' varsity and junior varsity volleyball teams need to check in

their uniform.

_____ **49.** The United Nations continue to have their headquarters in New York City.

_____ **50.** After their tai chi session, all of they were feeling refreshed and more relaxed.

Using Pronouns Correctly: Nominative, Objective, and Possessive Case; Clear Reference

A. CHOOSING CORRECT PRONOUN FORMS AND IDENTIFYING CASE Underline the correct pronoun form in parentheses in each of the following sentences. Then, indicate the case of the pronoun by writing above it *NOM* for *nominative*, *OBJ* for *objective*, or *POS* for *possessive*.

Example 1. Mrs. Olin told (*we*, <u>*us*</u>) the story of 18 Rabbit.
                                    OBJ

1. At first, we were all amused by (*him*, *his*) having such an odd name.

2. We soon discovered that (*he*, *him*) was no joke and had actually been a powerful Mayan ruler.

3. "Have any of you heard of (*him*, *he*) and his achievements?" Mrs. Olin asked.

4. Ellen had read about 18 Rabbit, so the only one who knew much about him was (*her*, *she*).

5. As the thirteenth governor of the Copán dynasty, (*he*, *him*) created a mighty empire in what is now Honduras.

6. His enemies feared him because he showed (*they*, *them*) little mercy.

7. However, 18 Rabbit's other achievements are primarily why historians recognize (*he*, *him*) as a great leader.

8. They have given (*his*, *him*) the title "King of the Arts."

9. What most ensured (*his*, *him*) being remembered down through the ages were the lasting monuments he ordered built in Copán.

10. Enemies from another city finally ambushed the old ruler, who was killed by (*they*, *them*), ending his rule after forty-three years.

B. CHOOSING CORRECT PRONOUN FORMS Underline the correct pronoun form in parentheses in each of the following sentences.

Example 1. It is up to the judges, Arnold and (*she*, <u>*her*</u>), to make a decision.

11. Didn't you sell more tickets than (*he*, *him*), Joel?

12. The book was written by James Lee, (*who*, *whom*) is also an editor.

13. The principal named two winners, Chris and (*me*, *I*).

14. After the game on Saturday, Joey and (*I*, *me*) went over to his house.

15. Did Carlos say (*whom*, *who*) the safety officer will be?

16. Tiffany usually rides to school on the bus with Carrie and (*I*, *me*).

17. Before class we talked to Janelle, (*who*, *whom*) Mr. Barry assigned to our study group last week.

18. No, (*we*, *us*) sophomores always sit on the other side of the gym.

19. The parking lot attendant gave (*they, them*) the receipt.

20. When Jenny and (*myself, I*) saw the kitten, both of us wanted it.

C. PROOFREADING SENTENCES FOR CORRECT PRONOUN FORMS Most of the following sentences contain at least one pronoun that has been used incorrectly. Draw a line through each incorrect pronoun, and write the correct form above it. If a sentence is already correct, write *C* on the line provided.

Example _____ **1.** Harold, ~~who~~ you haven't met, will lend his DVD player to Tracy and ~~I~~.
(above "who": whom) *(above "I": me)*

_____ **21.** The coach told the team that they needed to concentrate more on them fielding.

_____ **22.** When I called Anne's house, I ended up talking to Gabriel instead of she.

_____ **23.** The guests of honor—Phillip and her—were surprised when they walked into the party.

_____ **24.** "Whom do you say should clean up the living room?" Frieda asked.

_____ **25.** Do you drink herbal tea as often as us?

_____ **26.** The Italian quartet entertained us for almost two hours.

_____ **27.** Marissa gave Rose and myself a copy of the new schedule.

_____ **28.** Mr. Gray and her appointed two new squad leaders, she and I.

_____ **29.** You can give they the chemicals for the chemistry lab experiment.

_____ **30.** If these skates are yours, then where are my?

_____ **31.** Raymond, who I saw at the theater, likes acting as much as I.

_____ **32.** Although my uncle Paul and them are going to the game, Dad is not.

_____ **33.** "If Aaron doesn't trust even himself to do the job, whom does he trust?" Karen asked.

_____ **34.** Yes, I recall that the cat lost hers mittens, but do you recall whom found them?

_____ **35.** The judge offered we jurors a chance to ask him questions about his instructions.

_____ **36.** Besides Samantha, whom has competed in the bike rodeo?

_____ **37.** Are you and him working together on reorganizing the bulletin board?

_____ **38.** "Just between you and I," Allen said, "I don't think their idea will work, do you?"

_____ **39.** Only the doctors themselves could evaluate my stepsister's X-rays, which she had brought with her from the clinic.

_____ **40.** Yes, it really was us who played better than them.

D. CORRECTING UNCLEAR PRONOUN REFERENCE On the line provided, revise each of the following sentences to correct each unclear pronoun reference.

Example 1. Bill asked Michael to hand him his glass.

Bill asked Michael for Michael's glass.

41. Mary fixed my flat tire and didn't charge me anything for it.

_____

42. Henry met Wally when he worked at the grocery store.

_____

43. I'm riding home with them after school, which should be quicker.

_____

44. In the ad, it lists bananas for only twenty cents a pound.

_____

45. Andrew lost the first game, but that didn't upset him.

_____

46. Ms. Evans is very talented, and one of them is playing the guitar.

_____

47. Linda talked to Twila while she was folding the wash.

_____

48. When Grandma was sixteen, you could buy gas for fifty cents a gallon.

_____

49. Stan received his first check yesterday; that is why he was happy.

_____

50. After assisting with the computer programming, Lu decided to become one.

_____

Using Verbs Correctly: Principal Parts, Tense, Voice, and Mood

A. PROOFREADING SENTENCES FOR CORRECT VERB FORMS Most of the following sentences contain at least one error in the use of verbs. Draw a line through each incorrect verb form, and write the correct form above it. If a sentence is already correct, write *C* on the line provided.

Example _____ **1.** Nicholas ~~lay~~ *laid* the book on the table and then ~~set~~ *sat* down in the chair.

_____ **1.** When we lived near Quebec, we use to ice-skate on the pond when it freezed thick enough each year.

_____ **2.** The wind begun to howl sometime after midnight, so I got up and closed the window.

_____ **3.** The nurse sended you a note today to remind you to pick up your new glasses.

_____ **4.** The pen pals from Japan and Iceland had wrote to each other for years before they actually met.

_____ **5.** Phyllis sayed that she has rose every morning at five o'clock for years.

_____ **6.** The girl had dreamed of a house that looked much like this one.

_____ **7.** I seen you last night at the video store.

_____ **8.** She has took the papers to be recycled.

_____ **9.** They were suppose to have gave me a map.

_____ **10.** Set, Spark, and wait there until I get back.

_____ **11.** I done everything you telled me to.

_____ **12.** Tony drew a picture of a Spanish mission he had seen when he spent last summer in California.

_____ **13.** Jake rided the donkey from the corral to the house.

_____ **14.** No one cares if you have wore that shirt before.

_____ **15.** Mack and his stepdad raised the heavy board above their heads and set it carefully on top of the shed.

_____ **16.** Mr. Carlson teached at Riverside High before he come to our school.

_____ **17.** After Jodie breaked the vase, she sat the pieces on the shelf.

_____ **18.** Have you drank all the lemonade and ate all the sandwiches yet?

_____ **19.** After we had drove nearly all morning, we finally got to the beach and swum for an hour before we ate lunch.

_____ **20.** Please lie the grocery sacks on the counter.

B. USING THE DIFFERENT TENSES OF VERBS In each of the following sentences, change the tense of the verb to the tense indicated in parentheses. Underline the original verb form, and write the new form above it.

will have been riding

Example 1. The tired sisters <u>have ridden</u> on a train for five hours. (*future perfect progressive*)

21. Yes, they have gone to the awards banquet again this year. (*future*)

22. The infielders threw the ball around to each other as part of their warm-up routine.

(*past progressive*)

23. In the fall my grandfather will rake the leaves from these trees into a huge pile. (*present*)

24. The president had spoken at the luncheon in honor of Mexican American business owners.

(*past*)

25. Jane renewed her subscription to the magazine in time for the February issue. (*future perfect*)

26. The hostess will ask about our seating preference. (*past emphatic*)

27. Mr. Snow began graduate school this past summer. (*past perfect*)

28. We talked before dinner about our Sioux heritage. (*past perfect progressive*)

29. We shop for the best bargains, often at thrift stores. (*present perfect*)

30. The lecture appeals to Joe's interest in Latin America. (*present emphatic*)

C. PROOFREADING FOR CONSISTENCY OF TENSE Most of the following sentences contain errors in the use of tenses. Draw a line through an incorrect verb form, and write the correct form above it. If a sentence is already correct, write *C* on the line provided.

got

Example _____ **1.** The singer quickly left the arena and ~~gets~~ into his car.

_____ **31.** Pete is still in speech class this week, but tomorrow he has switched to drama.

_____ **32.** The sports announcer visited our school and will talk about baseball legends such as

Hank Aaron.

_____ **33.** Dorothy informed me that it is raining now.

_____ **34.** Yesterday we ate burritos for lunch and then make enchiladas for supper.

_____ **35.** The Franco-Prussian War started in 1870 but lasts only to 1871.

D. WRITING APPROPRIATE MODALS For each of the following sentences, supply an appropriate modal. Do not use the same modal more than once.

Example 1. They _____*must*_____ have been aware of the petitions.

36. The salesclerk said that the store definitely _____ honor the coupons.

37. You _____ skip today's practice, if you want.

38. "_____ you have any questions, just call me," Dr. Janssen said.

39. Nobody _____ figure out the solution to the mystery.

40. Nadia _____ move to Jamaica next year to be near her family.

E. IDENTIFYING ACTIVE AND PASSIVE VOICE Identify whether the verb in each of the following sentences is in the active or the passive voice. On the line provided, write *AV* for *active voice* or *PV* for *passive voice*.

Example _*PV*_ **1.** The books were published by a small press in Italy.

_____ **41.** To our amazement, both houses were sold immediately.

_____ **42.** The decision was made by the full tribal council, not just the elders.

_____ **43.** The horse jumped the fence on the west side of the barn.

_____ **44.** Mint is frequently found in herb gardens.

_____ **45.** Joan and Evan save brochures for their scrapbooks.

F. IDENTIFYING MOOD FORMS OF VERBS Identify the mood of the italicized verb in each of the following sentences. On the line provided, write *IND* for *indicative*, *IMP* for *imperative*, or *SUB* for *subjunctive*.

Example _*SUB*_ **1.** The neighbors *could* at least *try* to be quieter.

_____ **46.** If I *were* older, I could get a driver's license.

_____ **47.** We *believe* that the quiz team will do well.

_____ **48.** Please *respond* to the letter soon.

_____ **49.** *Can* you *tell* me who was the first woman senator?

_____ **50.** I had hoped that I *would be* able to help.

Using Modifiers Correctly: Forms, Comparison, and Placement

A. IDENTIFYING ADJECTIVE AND ADVERB MODIFIERS   Identify whether each of the underlined words, phrases, or clauses in the following sentences is used as an adjective or an adverb. On the line provided, write *ADJ* for *adjective* or *ADV* for *adverb*. Then, circle the word or words that are modified.

Example   _ADV_   **1.** Despite the unexpected problems, everything (is going) well now.

_____ **1.** *Porgy and Bess* is the opera <u>that will play at the auditorium next week</u>.

_____ **2.** I hope that we can see that new movie <u>soon</u>.

_____ **3.** Ella was working <u>to earn extra money for a car</u>.

_____ **4.** Do you want to climb into the boat <u>first</u>, or shall I?

_____ **5.** The situation looked <u>bad</u>, but not hopeless.

_____ **6.** Jane did <u>not</u> know the answer when Mr. Smith called on her in class.

_____ **7.** The water here, which comes from a well, tastes <u>terrific</u>.

_____ **8.** When it comes to mountain climbing, Cory is a <u>real</u> pro.

_____ **9.** These moccasins, which are <u>very</u> sturdy, were made by American Indians.

_____ **10.** The silly duck really wanted to get <u>into the house</u> for some reason.

_____ **11.** Mandy dances well, considering she <u>just</u> started taking lessons.

_____ **12.** Cormac isn't the <u>only</u> Siamese cat Beth has; she has six others.

_____ **13.** <u>Before the storm hits</u>, we should take down the bird feeders.

_____ **14.** The movers parked their van <u>in front of our house</u> and began unloading it.

_____ **15.** The new printer, <u>which was installed last week</u>, produces clean copies.

_____ **16.** Did the <u>slow</u> turtle really beat the speedy rabbit?

_____ **17.** *Hasta mañana* means "see you tomorrow" <u>in Spanish</u>.

_____ **18.** Several of the students were sick last week, but now they are <u>well</u>.

_____ **19.** <u>Poised on the edge of her chair</u>, the harpist played her solo.

_____ **20.** The beginning of the game was really <u>slow</u>, but the pace quickened later.

B. PROOFREADING SENTENCES FOR THE CORRECT USE OF MODIFIERS   Each of the following sentences contains an error in the use of modifiers. To correct each sentence, draw a line through the error and, where necessary, write the correction above the error. If a sentence requires only the addition of a word or words, use a caret (∧) to show where the word or words should be inserted.

Example 1. The knight was ~~confidenter~~ as he approached the castle.
  more confident

21. The damage from the storm is worser here than it is farther inland.

22. The price of the furniture is lesser than we had expected.

23. We're always looking for the efficientest way to run the business.

24. Mom feeds the dog more often than any of the rest of us in the family.

25. Irene usually arrives earlier than anyone in her class.

26. The Celtic band is the liveliest one of the two bands that have made it to the final playoff.

27. That architect's proposal for the new Hindu temple is the less costly of the three that have been submitted.

28. The sky began clearing this afternoon and is supposed to be more clearer tomorrow.

29. My cold feels badder today than it did yesterday.

30. The blueberries in your basket are bluer than my basket.

31. Our family eats fast food least frequently now than we used to.

32. All of the choices on the breakfast menu looked so good that I couldn't decide which one I wanted more.

33. Even though the lake is less calmer than it was earlier, we can still go water-skiing.

34. Polly is usually more happier than I am.

35. Aaron's was the more entertaining bar mitzvah party of the many we've attended.

36. Your dog barks louder than any dog I've ever heard.

37. We're the most healthiest now than we've ever been.

38. The Navajo reservation is fartherer from here than I had thought it was.

39. We listened to the speaker more attentively than Francis.

40. "That movie had the surprisingest ending I've ever seen," Emily told the three of us.

C. CORRECTING DANGLING AND MISPLACED MODIFIERS Most of the following sentences contain dangling or misplaced modifiers. On the line provided, revise each incorrect sentence so that its meaning is clear. If the sentence is already correct, write *C* on the line provided.

Example 1. We heard the news about the president listening to the radio.

Listening to the radio, we heard the news about the president.

41. While surfing the Web, the electricity went off.

_____

42. Determined, the dense jungle ahead did not discourage the explorers.

_____

43. We only said that we would be able to help for a couple of hours.

_____

44. Dad sent his fishing rod back to the manufacturer that had broken.

_____

45. Glancing at the paper, the headline surprised me.

_____

46. We found out how to load software on page three of the manual.

_____

47. You could borrow my laptop to write your report.

_____

48. While waiting in the rain at the bus stop, my papers became soaked.

_____

49. Peggy knocked the glass off the shelf hurrying to answer the telephone.

_____

50. The police directed traffic around the car in the road that had stalled.

_____

A Glossary of Usage: Common Usage Problems

A. IDENTIFYING CORRECT USAGE In each of the following sentences, underline the word or expression in parentheses that is correct according to standard, formal usage.

Example 1. Carl is my friend (*who*, *which*) (*emigrated*, *immigrated*) from Sweden.

1. "Joan (*taught*, *learned*) me a few things about the Vietnamese culture," Ray said.

2. Who (*beside*, *besides*) us will go to the convalescent home Saturday?

3. The pen that I borrowed (*off*, *from*) you is here somewhere.

4. Do you know who (*discovered*, *invented*) the first computer chip?

5. Few of the employees will be (*affected*, *effected*) by the new changes (*what*, *that*) have occurred.

6. Most of the audience liked the drummer (*alot*, *a lot*), but some didn't.

7. I heard on the radio (*where*, *that*) Mullins Street will be closed for a month.

8. We probably won't be able to go to the arcade today (*unless*, *without*) my cousin Dave drives us over there.

9. What were you (*implying*, *inferring*) when you said that?

10. The elephant (*who*, *that*) sometimes sprays water on visitors was not out this morning.

11. The jury talked (*between*, *among*) themselves a few more minutes before answering the judge.

12. Mom and Aunt Laura caught (*fewer*, *less*) fish today than they did yesterday.

13. Sharon's father is (*kind of*, *rather*) nostalgic about San Francisco because he (*use to*, *used to*) live there.

14. During the play the lighting, sound effects, and fog machine created the (*allusion*, *illusion*) of a stormy night.

15. It's been quite (*a while*, *awhile*) since we've had pasta.

16. The others are (*all ready*, *already*) for the party, but I'm not.

17. All of the class (*accept*, *except*) Travis and Julie have finished the assignment.

18. My aunt and uncle were (*suppose to*, *supposed to*) be here by now.

19. Did you notice the story's (*allusion*, *illusion*) that Carrie likes best?

20. Leland (*accepted*, *excepted*) the praise and considered (*hisself*, *himself*) fortunate.

21. Stacy's brother is older (*than*, *then*) she is, but her sisters are younger.

22. "Those (*kind*, *kinds*) of shops are usually interesting," Elena said.

23. I wish my parents would (*leave, let*) me go with you this weekend.

24. No one can predict what (*affect, effect*) longer life spans will have on our society.

25. Jackie said he (*don't, doesn't*) remember who (*borrowed, lent*) him a pencil yesterday.

B. PROOFREADING FOR CORRECT USAGE   Most of the following sentences contain at least one error in the use of formal, standard English. Draw a line through each error, and when necessary, write the correct word or words above the error. Also, replace any gender-specific words or expressions with nonsexist ones. Be sure to check for correct capitalization and punctuation after you correct each sentence. If the sentence is already correct, write *C* on the line provided.

Example _____ **1.** Dr. Ray's advice had a tremendous ~~affect~~ *effect* on my life, and I won't ~~hardly~~

forget what he said.

_____ **26.** Mankind has come a long ways in many respects, I believe.

_____ **27.** Hopefully, they remembered to bring their coats with them when they left here a few

minutes ago.

_____ **28.** On the walking tour, we saw many historic buildings, such as churches, private homes,

inns, and etc.

_____ **29.** Martha don't know where the headquarters of the NAACP is at.

_____ **30.** There wasn't no way they could of predicted what would happen.

_____ **31.** Chicago is all the farther this here plane goes, isn't it?

_____ **32.** The children were not suppose to be jumping off of the wall.

_____ **33.** "Try and see that Luis Valdez play, if its still playing," Mr. Carr recommended.

_____ **34.** The reason Jack doesn't want to move to a apartment is because he likes his big yard.

_____ **35.** Washing them small cars is a one-man operation.

_____ **36.** "You hadn't ought to leave the grass get so high before you mow it," Jordan said.

_____ **37.** A number of my ancestors emigrated from Germany.

_____ **38.** Being as you have American Indian grandparents, you may be able to help

Ms. Gonzalez with information for the American history project.

_____ **39.** Andy busted his pocket watch when he fell on the ice last night.

_____ **40.** That stapler takes this kind of a refill, not any of them kinds.

_____ **41.** If I had of seen you at the gym, we could have exercised together a while.

_____ **42.** Karla, my cousin, which recently returned from Europe, visited several countries

beside England.

_____ **43.** Have you noticed that many theme parks have rides and other attractions that try to

create the allusion that you're somewheres else in time or space?

_____ **44.** My neighbor asked if she could borrow a cup of plant food off of my mom.

_____ **45.** Many Mexican Americans they celebrate the ceremony of *Las Posadas*.

_____ **46.** "It's alright if the job takes a bit longer then we had planned," Lynn said.

_____ **47.** The girls never said nothing that would infer that they were not satisfied with the

results.

_____ **48.** Dad said he ain't able to read the odometer without he uses his new glasses.

_____ **49.** The guidance counselor explained that *proctoring* is when someone supervises an

academic exam.

_____ **50.** We were encouraged some when we found out that their going to be on our team.

Capitalization: Standard Uses of Capitalization

A. USING CAPITAL LETTERS CORRECTLY   In the following sentences, underline each word that should begin with a capital letter.

Example 1. In his autobiographical book titled *rocket boys*, homer hickam tells about how he
          made his boyhood dream come true.

1. after being listed as a bestseller in *the new york times*, hickam's book was made into a movie called *october sky*.

2. The book and the movie focus on the author's early life in coalwood, west virginia.

3. during the space race between the united states and the former soviet union, hickam dreamed of being a rocket scientist.

4. he and his friends launched a number of rockets and eventually won a gold medal at the national science fair.

5. a bigger dream came true when hickam grew up to become an engineer with the national aeronautics and space administration (nasa).

6. his book started as an article for *smithsonian air and space magazine*.

7. the article immediately attracted the attention of new york publishers and hollywood filmmakers.

8. starring in the movie is jake gyllenhaal, who plays the teenage homer.

9. also in the film is laura dern as an inspiring teacher, miss riley.

10. the movie takes its name from the turning point in hickam's life when he first saw the russian satellite *sputnik* in october 1957 and decided then to start building rockets.

B. PROOFREADING FOR THE CORRECT USE OF CAPITAL LETTERS   In each of the following sentences, circle any lowercase letters that should be capitalized, and draw a line through any capital letters that should be lowercase.

Example 1. The spokesperson for republic bank said, "We are a Democratic institution, one of the finest on Earth.

1. Dora was born on the last friday in january during the severest Winter we have ever had.

2. When aunt Iris called on my Birthday, she said that earth and mars were at their closest point in years.

3. The playwright wrote, "now, o Helen, glance this way."

14. Former major league Umpire steve palermo helps raise money to support the national paralysis foundation.

15. To foster the growth of their economies, the nations of europe have formed an association known as the european economic community.

16. at the korean restaurant, i ordered pickled radishes and black beans.

17. James was hired by the U.S. department of Agriculture to help teach farmers in Developing Countries about crop rotation.

18. The catalog for goodyear tires was sent to our old address, 959 Adams avenue.

19. The englewood theater is a beautiful building that dates from the 1940s.

20. My main Reference Source, *africana*, is subtitled *the encyclopedia of the african and african american experience*.

21. have you read Nora's new poem, titled "while the carousel spins"?

22. The first manned expedition to the moon was *apollo 8*, which was launched from Kennedy space center in cape canaveral, Florida.

23. Wasn't it dr. Blevins who discussed the taoist ideas about Work and Creativity?

24. My sister's college courses include geography I, Music, German, and Journalism.

25. Frank's new dog, king, looks like a boston bull, but it's not a purebred.

26. The mount rushmore national memorial is in south Dakota, isn't it?

27. In our class poll, president Lincoln topped the list of most admired Presidents.

28. Yes, portuguese is one of four official Languages of latin america.

29. My Dad signs even his e-mail messages "sincerely Yours."

30. The scottish dancers literally stopped the show last night.

C. CORRECTING ERRORS IN CAPITALIZATION Some of the following items contain errors in capitalization. Correct each error by rewriting the item on the line provided. If an item is already correct, write *C* on the line.

Example 1. the summer solstice festival _____*the Summer Solstice Festival*_____

31. department of education _____

32. for you, mayor _____

33. groundhog day _____

34. a chickasaw tradition _____

35. a plymouth minivan _____

36. Shakespeare's play *much ado about nothing* _____

37. Irma and her cat Missy _____

38. the battle of tippecanoe _____

39. 2909 State st. _____

40. dear ms. Ford: _____

41. the greek god poseidon _____

42. at castle medical center _____

43. the kansas city chiefs _____

44. Orizaba, Mexico's highest mountain _____

45. Ronald J. Sears, ph.d. _____

46. a nobel prize _____

47. biology II, speech, and French _____

48. the peruvian culture _____

49. your Cousin Ernie _____

50. Chapter 1, pp. 5–30 _____

Punctuation: End Marks and Commas

A. **CORRECTING SENTENCES BY ADDING END MARKS** Insert end marks (periods, exclamation points, and question marks) where they are needed in the following sentences.

Example **1.** He asked if we had recently heard from Madison.

1. After we moved into the apartment, we painted the living room yellow

2. Do you have an e-mail address for your cousin in Singapore

3. What an awesome view that is

4. Please let me know when you want to borrow the Paul Theroux books

5. What happened to the political prisoners in the former Soviet Union after the collapse of the communist government there

6. My aunt has asked me to check the Internet for local stock prices for her

7. Do your best

8. Martin told me that Mark Twain was one of the first authors who created their work on a typewriter

9. Can you imagine doing without electricity and motorized transportation

10. Well, I suppose people back then managed without them, and I guess that we could, too

B. **USING ABBREVIATIONS CORRECTLY** On the line provided, rewrite each of the following sentences, correcting any errors in the use of abbreviations. If a sentence is already correct, write *C* on the line.

Example **1.** We read Homer last Dec. to find out what life was like in BC 800.

We read Homer last December to find out what life was like in 800 B.C.

11. This recipe for shortbread calls for two tsps. of ginger and makes three one-lb. loaves.

_____

12. Mrs. Harrison assigned us two poems by A. E. Housman.

_____

13. Do you know the most important event of 1600 A.D. in Asia?

_____

14. The Internal Revenue Service (I.R.S.) has issued new procedures for filing tax returns.

_____

15. Sen. Nowells asked for a full environmental study of the proposed building.

_____

ELEMENTS OF LANGUAGE | Fourth Course

16. We should arrive in New Hope, Pa, about PM 6:00.

_____

17. Our new garage measures twenty feet by thirty feet.

_____

18. The marathon will be on the second Sat. in Sept.

_____

19. The veterinarian who examined the cat was Dr Tina Diamond, DVM.

_____

20. Our teacher, Ms Ames, is engaged to William R James, Junior.

_____

C. CORRECTING SENTENCES BY ADDING COMMAS Insert commas where they are needed in the following sentences. If a sentence is already correct, write C on the line provided.

Example _____ **1.** These shoes are too small; after I return them, I'll buy a larger pair, I imagine.

_____ **21.** Nancy would you please show Eric our new choir member where the music books are?

_____ **22.** Allen Lee not Adam Lee lives at 703 Post Street Coral Gables Florida.

_____ **23.** The Rays' house will sell quickly because the price is reasonable because its location is convenient and because it is spacious.

_____ **24.** Tomorrow we plan to rent the movie *Patch Adams*.

_____ **25.** Jody was looking forward to the quiz show yet he also felt nervous.

_____ **26.** "Don't waste your money on that dumb boring awful movie," Andrew said.

_____ **27.** Your magnolias Mr. Karney look especially bright and colorful after the rain this morning.

_____ **28.** Raised in Seattle Sue Ellen wondered what it would be like to live in New Orleans.

_____ **29.** No I can't go to the museum today and I probably won't be able to go tomorrow.

_____ **30.** The neighbors who were first to greet us the day we moved into our new house were Mr. and Mrs. Baylor.

_____ **31.** On the beach near our house in Florida children frequently build sand castles.

_____ **32.** The principal is at a convention; when she returns I'll tell her that you called.

_____ **33.** My twin brother and I were born on July 4 1990 after all.

_____ **34.** Wild turkeys which are large heavy birds sometimes fly when startled.

_____ **35.** Exhausted the volleyball champs collapsed onto the benches.

_____ **36.** As we discovered the trail through the woods not the one along the shore was the easier route.

_____ **37.** Asking for a rematch the coach remained calm but firm.

_____ **38.** From this far back in the auditorium we'll be able to hear the actors and actresses on stage, won't we?

_____ **39.** The pie could be made with cherries peaches apples or apricots.

_____ **40.** My friend Tim Clancy works at his mom and dad's pizza shop and in fact usually delivers our pizza whenever we order one.

_____ **41.** "Well the game was exciting but our team lost," Janey said.

_____ **42.** Tommy Gill M.D. moved to Cedarville in September of 1987.

_____ **43.** The ranchers decided that the old fence posts had to be replaced.

_____ **44.** Stephen Baker Jr. a banker has been elected mayor.

_____ **45.** When you come to the bend in the road where Mr. Johnson's property ends and the wildlife preserve begins turn left.

D. IDENTIFYING UNNECESSARY COMMAS Circle each comma that is unnecessary in the following sentences. If a sentence is already correct, write *C* on the line provided.

Example _____ **1.** My aunt, Pat, is staying with Cousin Pete, and helping him with his new business, a candle shop.

_____ **46.** As soon as she got home, Irene shut the front door, and opened the windows.

_____ **47.** Sometime in the morning, on Saturday, my best friend Angela and I are going to practice, our tennis serves, if it doesn't rain.

_____ **48.** The ticket seller asked Fred, a shy boy, if he had ever gone out on an offshore, fishing boat, before.

_____ **49.** Anyone, wanting a ride to soccer practice this afternoon, can come to my house, which is at 430, Elm Street.

_____ **50.** In most of the movie, the lead actor deliberately overplays the part, I think, and is really funny.

Punctuation: Semicolons and Colons

A. USING SEMICOLONS CORRECTLY IN SENTENCES Insert semicolons where they are needed in the following sentences. If a comma is already in a sentence where a semicolon should go, delete the comma and write the semicolon above it.

Example 1. Dr. New, a scientist; Mr. Cobbs, a teacher; and Mrs. Honeycutt, a health administrator, will be on the panel.

1. The driver's license test will be given on Saturday, April 3, Monday, April 5, Thursday, April 8, and Saturday, April 10.

2. Tiffany was wearing a nice sweater today in fact, it was one of the prettiest I've ever seen.

3. Hawaii Volcanoes National Park is on the island of Hawaii both volcanoes there, Mauna Loa and Kilauea, are active.

4. The lineup for the high school team is Lance Jameson, quarterback, Ben Trammel, end, and Bobby Dale, halfback.

5. They could go with Delilah, Jim, or Elaine, and Debby, Sandra, and Lynn could go with us.

6. Sara's hands were dry and itching consequently, she used an aloe vera hand cream.

7. Maria finally chose the purple gloves, not the green ones, which were the ones I would have chosen, but when she saw how much they cost, she put them back.

8. Our plan was to drive to the Pacific Ocean while in the Mexican state of Chiapas however, the car overheated and so we were forced to turn around.

9. The weather is getting colder it may be freezing by early afternoon.

10. Barbara's parents have lived in Anchorage, Alaska, Bombay, India, and Detroit, Michigan.

11. My dogs Ralph, Brownie, and Punkin, and Furry and Patches, the cats, seem to get along.

12. "These games are too expensive besides, I have most of them anyway," Neal said.

13. You sometimes hear people say *au contraire* that expression is French for "on the contrary."

14. Bill's mother is coming to pick us up she said she would be here at noon.

15. Walking to school, we saw a dog, a raccoon, and a squirrel, and Ada, my sister, also saw a turtle.

16. The Thai restaurant serves a curry dish with rice, vegetables, and coconut milk, a mixed vegetable dish including carrots, broccoli, and squash, and a shrimp dish with mushrooms, squash, and other vegetables.

17. Cooked oatmeal is not good after it gets cold therefore, I eat it immediately.

18. Ann said she received only one piece of mail today it was her confirmation to go to computer

camp for a week this summer.

19. In our immediate family, there are birthdays on October 13, 1935, October 13, 1972, and

October 13, 1990.

20. Let's watch for Myra, Lane, and Richard, and Ben and Frances can be on the lookout for the

others.

B. USING COLONS IN CONVENTIONAL SITUATIONS On the line provided, rewrite each of the following
items, inserting colons where they are needed.

Example 1. II Chronicles 2 1–10   *II Chronicles 2: 1-10* _____

21. Dear Miss Poole   _____

22. List the following lions, tigers, bears   _____

23. Exodus 40 1–12   _____

24. 6 30 in the morning   _____

25. Dear General Armstrong   _____

26. the 7 00 P.M. train   _____

27. "Beware Do Not Read This Poem"   _____

28. after sunset at 8 30   _____

29. Acts 17 28–29   _____

30. *African American Life A Modern Portrait*   _____

C. PROOFREADING FOR SEMICOLONS AND COLONS IN SENTENCES Insert semicolons and colons where
they are needed in the following sentences. If an item is already correct, write *C* on the line provided.

Example _____ **1.** A new method for making building blocks uses the following materials**:**

shredded used paper, sand, water, and cement**;** the blocks are used in

house construction.

_____ **31.** "We have to be in class by 7 45 A.M., or we're tardy," Wayne said.

_____ **32.** We must act now we can do it!

_____ **33.** First, we will discuss the functions of the House of Representatives next, we will look

at the duties of the Senate.

_____ **34.** Here is an interesting fact New York City and Madrid are at almost the same latitude.

_____ **35.** John 3 16 is one of the most widely quoted verses from the Bible.

_____ **36.** The mayor concluded his speech with these words The time is here when the city must take a stand for the future of its children. We must commit to stricter laws that help preserve the earth and each other, even if this commitment requires changes in our lifestyles.

_____ **37.** The art show features an unusual painting called *Day Lilies A Night View.*

_____ **38.** Last week Erma bought a dress, a blouse, and two scarves and a coat, shoes, and a belt were given to her.

_____ **39.** This morning around 7:00 we began washing the following items: sheets, pillowcases, a comforter, and a thermal blanket.

_____ **40.** You might want to consider an outdoor job this summer for instance, you could apply to the county parks department or to landscaping companies," Ms. Sutherland told me.

_____ **41.** Dad likes the new furniture I think it's uncomfortable.

_____ **42.** The packages were coded as follows red, Benjamin blue, Matthew yellow, Karen and green, Geoffrey.

_____ **43.** When it is 5 30 P.M. in Barcelona, what time is it in Phoenix?

_____ **44.** Ned has a new job: He now is senior director of software sales.

_____ **45.** Last weekend we played tourists in our own city and visited the following sites the park, the old Spanish fort, the art museum, and the science museum.

_____ **46.** Crystal gave me a copy of her first book, *Crystal Clear My Story* it is quite enjoyable.

_____ **47.** Proverbs 6 6 combines humor and wisdom "Go to the ant, you lazybones; consider its ways, and be wise."

_____ **48.** Marty teamed up with Kim and Charlotte and Kate and Cindy teamed up with Judy.

_____ **49.** The history book says that Leonardo da Vinci was a Renaissance man He was a sculptor, painter, architect, and engineer.

_____ **50.** Touchdown locations on the flight were as follows Miami, Florida Houston, Texas and Los Angeles, California.

Punctuation: Italics, Quotation Marks, and Ellipsis Points

A. USING ITALICS (UNDERLINING) CORRECTLY IN SENTENCES Underline each item that should be italicized in each of the following sentences.

Example 1. According to this textbook, <u>Foundation Course in French</u>, the phrase <u>Qu'est-ce que</u>

<u>c'est?</u> means "What is it?"

1. Who played Dorothy in The Wizard of Oz?

2. Thumbing through Amtrak's timetable, I decided to ride the Texas Eagle to San Antonio.

3. Have you ever noticed that the prefix pre– appears in the word prefix?

4. I explained to my brother again what the symbols < and > mean.

5. Myths, heroes, and legends are at the core of Alfred, Lord Tennyson's epic poem Idylls of the King.

6. Cruise ships such as Amsterdam and Rhapsody of the Seas take passengers through the Panama Canal.

7. When someone sneezes, many people wish the person good health by saying the German word gesundheit.

8. Tom Brokaw, anchor of NBC News, is the author of The Greatest Generation.

9. After reading the play I Never Sang for My Father, we discussed the responsibilities of children for their parents.

10. One test question asked for the date the United States launched the space probe Voyager 2.

B. PUNCTUATING SENTENCES BY ADDING QUOTATION MARKS AND OTHER MARKS OF PUNCTUATION
In the following sentences, insert quotation marks, single quotation marks, and other marks of punctuation where they are needed. Circle any lowercase letters that should be capitalized. If a sentence is already correct, write C on the line provided.

Example _____ **1.** "I've heard," said Joan, "the saying, 'a stitch in time saves nine.'"

_____ **11.** What a beautiful apartment you have here Beth exclaimed in a small amount of space, you've done wonders.

_____ **12.** Carl said that his family may move back to Australia, but he hopes not.

_____ **13.** Over and over, the bandleader yelled one, two; one, two!

_____ **14.** I think said Darrell that the architect studied in Japan. I believe that I recognize traditional Japanese symbols in some of his designs.

_____ **15.** Did Jim Brown play football or baseball Myra asked.

_____ **16.** Our assignment tonight is to read the short story The Monkey's Paw, which I've read

twice before.

_____ **17.** Joshua said Millie came up to me and asked are you going?

_____ **18.** Tom calls himself an e-hawk because he spends so much time checking e-mail.

_____ **19.** Did Shawn really say, "The trees must be saved"?

_____ **20.** Have you memorized Countee Cullen's poem Sonnet asked Lin.

_____ **21.** When thanking someone, many people use the phrase No problem I wonder why

they say that instead of "You're welcome."

_____ **22.** I think the first chapter of the book is titled either "In the Beginning, I" or "I, at the

Beginning."

_____ **23.** How many times has she asked you Have you finished your homework

_____ **24.** Aaron said that he doesn't listen to much music but that he likes the song Let There

Be Peace on Earth.

_____ **25.** I'm trying to figure out Emily said if Ethan was telling the truth when he said Not me!

C. PUNCTUATING DIALOGUE BY ADDING QUOTATION MARKS   Add quotation marks where they belong
in the following dialogue. Insert a paragraph symbol (¶) wherever a new paragraph should begin.

Example   **[1]** "The new grocery store near the school is great!" Janis exclaimed. ¶"Yes, and the

bakery and the Italian oven are especially great," Wyatt said.

[26] Going to the bakery area is like taking a tour of the world. Breads from everywhere are not
_nly sold, but also baked right there in the store.   **[27]** I saw—and tasted—breads made the way
hey are in Italy, France, Mexico, South Africa, and India, Wyatt said.   **[28]** Did you read about the
_ven? Janis asked. Who built it?   **[29]** It's a wood-fired bread oven, Wyatt said, and it was built . . .
_0] You mean they actually burn wood inside the oven in the store? Janis interrupted.   **[31]** Yes,
_at's right. That oven can hold up to one hundred loaves at once.   **[32]** The oven maker is from
_arcelona, Spain. He's one of only a few people today who know how to build such a wood-fired
_read oven, Wyatt explained.   **[33]** Tell me, Janis said, about some of the breads.   **[34]** Wyatt
_nswered, My favorites are French baguettes and Italian cheese bread.   **[35]** You'll no doubt find
_ore than one favorite, too, Janis. Be sure to stop by the bakery next time you're at the new store.

D. USING ELLIPSIS POINTS CORRECTLY For each of the following passages, follow the directions in parentheses. On the lines provided, rewrite the sentences, using ellipsis points and end marks to punctuate each omission correctly.

Example 1. "Do you think there will ever be alternatives to gas-powered vehicles? *I think there will be.* Fossil fuels will run out sooner or later." (Omit the italicized sentence.)

"Do you think there will ever be alternatives to gas-powered vehicles?. . . Fossil fuels will run out sooner or later."

36. "Holidays are overrated, but well, I admit I do like Valentine's Day," Joyce said. (Indicate a pause between *but* and *well.*)

_____

37. The resort near Guadalajara *is a relaxing place with good meals and* has beautiful bathing pools o warm water. (Omit the italicized sentence part.)

_____

_____

38. The Shoji Tabuchi Show was a highlight of my trip to Branson, Missouri, *where I once lived as a child.* Shoji is a fabulous violinist, and his show is entertaining. (Omit the italicized sentence part.)

_____

_____

39. The people have spoken! *The will of the people will be done. Wrongs will be righted.* The vote was strongly in favor of the controversial proposal. (Omit the italicized part.)

_____

_____

40. Little dustings of snow

Usually come and go

But, as you already know

Sadly, this year's a no-show. (Omit the italicized part.)

_____

_____

_____

_____

Punctuation: Apostrophes, Hyphens, Dashes, Parentheses, Brackets

A. CORRECTING SENTENCES BY ADDING APOSTROPHES   Insert apostrophes where they are needed in the following sentences. If a sentence is already correct, write *C* on the line provided.

Example _____ **1.** Maybe Pat's idea of a fun time is to memorize facts, such as the names of all the states' capitals, but it's not mine.

_____ **1.** In small type, *3*s sometimes look like *8*s to me.

_____ **2.** The new contract means several more months work, doesnt it, Dad?

_____ **3.** Looking on the map, I searched the Indian Ocean east of Africa for Seychelles exact location.

_____ **4.** Mr. Bleacher recalled how much snow we had during the winter of 1990, but he said the winter of '92 was more severe.

_____ **5.** Everyones favorite story in the new childrens magazine is the one about the Cherokee girl and her flowers.

_____ **6.** A. L.s and Mikes bicycles are similar, but Mikes is older.

_____ **7.** To make the tenses consistent, I will change the *do*'s to *did*'s.

_____ **8.** The mices entrance may be under the sink, so I'll seal any openings there.

_____ **9.** My sister and brother-in-laws house is on two acres overlooking the Mississippi River.

_____ **10.** Brian's report card showed two As this semester—a 100 percent improvement.

_____ **11.** "Whos the joker who changed our departure time to five o clock?" Nan asked.

_____ **12.** While anybodys help would be appreciated, were especially hoping that we will get Carloss assistance.

_____ **13.** We tried for hours but couldn't get the program installed on Gus's computer.

_____ **14.** I dont know whose apple was left on my desk, but its gone now.

_____ **15.** My parents dont like to miss NPRs evening news program.

_____ **16.** The countries leaders met in Mexico City for their annual conference.

_____ **17.** "Lets take Marys and her advice," Joey pleaded.

_____ **18.** I brought my own skates, and Danielle brought hers, but Joel and Claire forgot to bring theirs.

_____ **19.** Teresas and Jeans new hairstyles are distinctive, but neithers cut appeals to me.

_____ **20.** The squirrels supply of acorns was enormous, so they had plenty to eat all winter.

B. USING HYPHENS TO DIVIDE WORDS AT THE ENDS OF LINES On the line provided, write each of the following words, using a hyphen to indicate where the word may be divided at the end of a line. If a word should not be divided, write *do not divide*.

Example 1. extremity _____ *ex-trem-i-ty* _____

21. mother-in-law _____

22. ginger _____

23. athletics _____

24. creation _____

25. locked _____

26. rehearse _____

27. African _____

28. reigns _____

29. self-control _____

30. necessary _____

C. USING HYPHENS, DASHES, PARENTHESES, AND BRACKETS Insert hyphens, dashes, parentheses, and brackets to punctuate the following sentences correctly. Use a caret (ʌ) to indicate where each hyphen and dash should go, and write the hyphen or dash above the line. Do not add commas to any sentence.

Example 1. "The youths couldn't miss the high‾water markʌ[8 feet]on the wall," the reporter said.

31. A record fifty nine students signed up to compete in the annual science fair.

32. The Amazon River is the second-longest river in the world. (See page 407 Map 2 for its route.)

33. "The game I know this will be a disappointment has been delayed an hour," Mr. Reynolds said.

34. We watched the amazing stunt fliers at least when we weren't blinded by the sun.

35. I am pleased to announce that the president elect is John Graham.

36. Three of the world's major religions Judaism, Christianity, and Islam began in Southwest Asia.

37. The concert was well attended thank goodness because a lot of planning went into it.

38. Louis said that his great grandmother turned eighty five on her birthday in mid June.

39. The all star band received a standing ovation.

40. The moderator noted, "The contestants have held two of the same positions state treasurer and lieutenant governor."

41. The pyramids of Egypt how I've longed to see them are monuments of mystery.

42. The recipe calls for only one third cup of honey.

43. "The project boy, do I have to get busy is due tomorrow," Sandy said.

44. The full length mirror on the closet door is quite handy.

45. Argentina has a varied landscape mountains, a plateau, a grassy plain, and forests.

46. Jawaharlal Nehru 1889–1964 was prime minister of India from 1947 to 1964.

47. "The well matched teams answered geography questions for two hours 1:00–3:00 P.M.,"
the show's producer said.

48. "Tune in next week for" the announcer was saying as Dad turned off the TV.

49. My uncle my mother's brother is a self educated businessman.

50. The books 7,500 of them were printed, weren't they? were trucked from the printer to
the publisher.

Spelling: Improving Your Spelling

A. PROOFREADING SENTENCES TO CORRECT SPELLING ERRORS Most of the following sentences contain at least one error in spelling or in the use of numbers. Cross out each error, and write the word or number correctly above the error. If a sentence is already correct, write *C* on the line provided.

                       safety   *superseded*

Example _____ **1.** The ~~safty~~ regulations ~~superceded~~ all other guidelines.

_____ **1.** While driveing on Interstate Ten yesterday, I noticed that the car's milage gauge is broken.

_____ **2.** Celestial phenomenons have intrigued humans for centurys.

_____ **3.** The three-years-olds were well behaved and surprisingly quiet.

_____ **4.** The arguement centered on how Tex-Mex food differs from authentic Mexican dishs.

_____ **5.** When you go to the grocery store, please buy 3 5-pound bags of cornmeal.

_____ **6.** Gliding effortlessly across the ice, the girls practiced their skating routines.

_____ **7.** Of the two scissorses, the kitchen pair was the one Martha always preferred.

_____ **8.** Were more potatos grown in Ireland or in Idaho in 1900?

_____ **9.** The 4th car on the frieght train was filled with grain.

_____ **10.** Perhaps you would like to know more about the believes of Tibetan Buddhists.

_____ **11.** The crys of the kittens echoed throughout the shelter even though fewwer cats than usual were there.

_____ **12.** All of the mens on the neighboring farms helped the Andersons rebuild thier barn that had been hit by the tornado.

_____ **13.** Do you consede that the proposed solution will create an even bigger problem?

_____ **14.** Yes, Lissa spells her name with two ss.

_____ **15.** Now that my sister is in college, she reads many contemporary essayes.

_____ **16.** Although the sculpture looked mishapen to me, it was one of two runner-ups for the grand prize.

_____ **17.** The lovely bowls made by the Zuni potters were decorated with figures of deer.

_____ **18.** "It's sunnyer now than it has been all day," Alice said happyly.

_____ **19.** When it snows heavily, niether the Lanes nor the Ramirezs like to shovel the sidewalks in front of their houses, so they take turns doing the whole stretch.

_____ **20.** All of the rodeoes were on Saturdaies last year, as I recall.

_____ **21.** Since Don loves aircrafts, his holiday card always has a picture of a plane.

_____ **22.** 3,000 people attended Odadaa's exceptionaly entertaining performance of music
from Ghana.

_____ **23.** The paper used to be a dayly, but now it is published 3 times a week.

_____ **24.** "Oh, these tomatos taste delicious!" Uncle Harry said.

_____ **25.** "I do beleive that the program exceded my expectations," Ms. Hull said.

DISTINGUISHING BETWEEN WORDS OFTEN CONFUSED Underline the correct word in each set of
parentheses in the following sentences.

Example 1. The election (all ready, already) has significantly (effected, affected) the states.

. It is more restful (than, then) we had expected (hear, here).

. "Is the (weather, whether) always this hot in the (dessert, desert)?" Li asked.

. When the choir was finally (all together, altogether), the practice began.

. The (principle, principal) at my school is greatly respected because she has such high
(principles, principals).

. The class refers to its newly married teacher as "the teacher (formally, formerly) known as
Miss Myers."

. Have you noticed how (your, you're) day brightens when you receive a (complement,
compliment)?

. Yes, everyone else in the class was (all ready, already) to go before I was.

. "Traffic tickets are a big (waist, waste) of money," Dad said.

. Would it be (all right, alright) if we missed rehearsal tonight?

. The sign read, "Be ready to use your (breaks, brakes)—you have just (passed, past) the
entrance to Wildlife Wonders!"

. Coach Saunders (led, lead) the students across the field this morning.

. All of the changes in the company have definitely had an (affect, effect) on the (moral, morale)
of employees.

. Nelson's grandfather worked as a coal (miner, minor) in West Virginia.

. With the economy booming, the board plans to add more (personal, personnel).

. (Their, There, They're) interested in buying (your, you're) baseball cards, I think.

. During Ed's first (coarse, course) in pottery, he made three beautiful bowls.

42. I'd like to go to Santiago someday because (its, it's) the (capital, capitol) of Chile.

43. The priest knelt at the (altar, alter) at the start of the (peace, piece) ceremony.

44. The movie has been (shone, shown) only one time all week long.

45. This (stationary, stationery) is from the office of the United States (consul, counsel) to Spain.

46. When did your uncle (loose, lose) his car keys?

47. (Who's, Whose) umbrella was left outside last night during the rain?

48. At the farmer's market yesterday, I (choose, chose) a kohlrabi, which looks similar (to, too) a cabbage.

49. Last summer the Chen family had (quiet, quite) a nice time visiting (their, there) relatives in San Francisco.

50. The guidance (councilor, counselor) gave them good advice.

Correcting Common Errors

A. Correcting Sentence Fragments and Run-on Sentences Identify each of the following word groups as a sentence fragment, run-on sentence, or complete sentence. On the line provided, write *F* for *fragment,* *R* for *run-on,* or *S* for a *complete sentence.* Correct each fragment by adding or deleting words to make a complete sentence. Correct each run-on by making it two separate sentences or one complete sentence. Use a caret (∧) to show where a word should be inserted. Punctuation and capitalization may also need to be changed.

Example __*R*__ **1.** Rice is the main dish in many Southeast Asian meals,∧ *and* other foods are served

simply to accompany the rice.

_____ **1.** If people can afford milled rice at all meals.

_____ **2.** Rice polished at a mill is called white rice, it is held in high regard by many Southeast

Asians because it has been processed.

_____ **3.** Some people who live far from a mill use mortars and pestles to pound their rice.

_____ **4.** In markets many kinds of rice are available.

_____ **5.** Guests usually receive white rice they might prefer unpolished rice, however.

_____ **6.** Like white rice better than brown rice?

_____ **7.** According to some people, better rice from the upland of Southeast Asia.

_____ **8.** Some rice is very flavorful; some rice is rather bland.

_____ **9.** Restaurants that serve Southeast Asian food, such as Thai and Vietnamese restaurants.

_____ **10.** Be sure to try the rice when you go to such a restaurant ask if the rice came from

Southeast Asia.

B. Correcting Usage Errors in Sentences Draw a line through the incorrect word or words in each of the following sentences. Then, when necessary, write the correct word or words above each error.

Example 1. The class was discussing the possibility of finding a ~~more~~ better place to have the

party for ~~she.~~ *her*

11. Students whom arrive early is supposed to arrange the chairs in rows and will clean the

chalkboard.

12. Neither Sharon nor Fern usually take their schoolbooks to the gym.

13. Dan and me will rise the garage door while you and him gets the lawn mower and the edger.

14. The Edmundsons use to go to the beach every weekend, but now they don't never go.

15. The pilot hisself navigated the ship perfect through the narrows and then set down to rest.

16. Please go with Juan and she to the store and get some milk, bread, eggs, and etc. for breakfast.

17. Tracy sung bad before someone gave she voice lessons last summer and learned her the scales.

18. The team are running up and down the bleachers as part of their training.

19. The news about the animals were a relief to the anxious visitors.

20. Either Joleen or her parents has already called about the lost dog, which was finded this morning.

21. Javier is one of them friends who always says the right thing.

22. The winners would have been them, if the game hadn't of been called because of rain.

23. Carla comes from a more bigger family than anyone in the class.

24. Several of hers songs have rose to the top of the charts this year.

25. The principal told the girls that he appreciated them pitching in to help with the open house.

26. The clowns—Elton and him—threw the ball back and forth.

27. "Everybody who want more popcorn should take his or her bowl up here," Ms. Hill said.

28. Sola, as well as her sisters, always perform real well on the ice rink.

29. Haven't you and your neighbors never had a fire drill at your apartment building?

30. Its a long ways to get to our new house, which is farthest from school than the apartment.

31. Someone must of set down on that there bench that had just been painted.

32. That is without doubt the comfortablest chair in the store, doesn't you agree?

33. Is it true that more then 30 percent of the population are considered to be "cultural creatives"?

34. Was any of the students pleased that the committee excepted the student council proposals?

35. "The longer I lay here, the least likely it becomes that I will go outside and work," Larry said.

C. REVISING SENTENCES TO CORRECT MISPLACED AND DANGLING MODIFIERS Each of the following sentences contains a misplaced or dangling modifier. Revise each sentence to correct the error.

Example 1. Becoming nervous, his knees began shaking.

Becoming nervous, he felt his knees begin shaking.

36. Is that your new cat next to the sofa with such long fur?

_____

37. Walking along the beach, the water looked inviting.

_____

38. They've almost given out the prizes to all of the winners.

_____

39. We saw your dog running down the street on the way to school.

_____

40. To succeed in business, discipline, direction, and dedication are necessary.

_____

D. CORRECTING MECHANICS ERRORS IN SENTENCES The following sentences contain errors in capitalization, punctuation, and spelling. Draw a line through each error, and write the correct word or punctuation mark in the space above the error. In some cases you will simply need to add or delete punctuation. Use a caret (∧) to show exactly where a hyphen or dash should go. Underline any words that should be in italics.

Example 1. Please procede with your plan an excellent one, by the way to decorate the capital for president's day, however, remember to stay within budget," mr. bloom said.

41. The jets, who havent won many games this spring have received a lot of criticism in last months issue of sports update.

42. compared to where we used to live the whether hear is extremly changable ben said although these seasonal cycles are normal arent they

43. Needing to refill there cupboard aunt ruth and uncle larry asked me to pick up the following groceries for them flour beans cereal and soup three different kinds

44. Dolores has worked hard to raise her grades in those two coarses french and algebra 1 this grading period and i think she did.

45. "The 9 45 A.M. train from chicago has all ready arrived exclaimed Patricia hurry or well miss it

46. The kitchen knifes were quiet dull consequently Michael volunteered to sharpen them.

47. Please see whose speaking at the rally tonight it may be general arnold one of the towns genuine heros

48. We need to make delivery's at 3 more towns near here 901 Main st Garland 312 First ave Euless and 150 Charlotte dr Bedford.

49. Our nieghbors japanese garden is the most peaceful place Ive ever been in my life.

50. "Some dogs probably ours have gotten into the trash" Sheila started to say but her words trailled off.